D1607547

The Student Athlete's Guide to College Success

The Student Athlete's Guide to College Success

Algerian Hart and F. Erik Brooks

GREENWOOD™

An Imprint of ABC-CLIO, LLC

Santa Barbara, California • Denver, Colorado

Library of Congress Cataloging-in-Publication Data

Names: Hart, Algerian, author. | Brooks, F. Erik., author.
Title: The student athlete's guide to college success / Algerian Hart and F.
    Erik Brooks.
Description: Santa Barbara, California : Greenwood, an Imprint of ABC-CLIO,
    LLC, [2017] | Includes bibliographical references and index.
Identifiers: LCCN 2016028020 (print) | LCCN 2016046697 (ebook) | ISBN
    9781440847035 (acid-free paper) | ISBN 9781440847042 (ebook)
Subjects: LCSH: College student orientation. | Academic achievement. |
    College athletes—Education.
Classification: LCC LB2343.3 .H387 2017 (print) | LCC LB2343.3 (ebook) |
    DDC378.1/98—dc23
LC record available at https://lccn.loc.gov/2016028020

ISBN: 978-1-4408-4703-5
EISBN: 978-1-4408-4704-2

21 20 19 18 17   1 2 3 4 5

This book is also available as an eBook.

Greenwood
An Imprint of ABC-CLIO, LLC

ABC-CLIO, LLC
130 Cremona Drive, P.O. Box 1911
Santa Barbara, California 93116-1911
www.abc-clio.com

This book is printed on acid-free paper ∞
Manufactured in the United States of America

Contents

Introduction

Many high school student athletes have fantasized of competing in March Madness, the Bowl Championship Series Bowl Game, or the College World Series. They have grown up dreaming of having their big play shown over and over on *Sports Center* or other sports shows. High school student athletes see the lure and prestige of big time college athletics, and it is very enticing. However, for the majority of high school athletes who continue their athletic career and compete on the college level, they will not compete on national television or get the notoriety from their highlights being seen on ESPN or Fox Sports. Only the best of the best will make it to play professional sports. With this reality, the opportunity to receive a college education should be among the goals of accepting an athletic scholarship. The recruiting process is very different depending on the sport and the division for which a student is being recruited. Unlike the money allocated for scholarships, the amount of money spent on recruiting is not regulated. As students are being recruited, they will discover that some programs, particularly large-revenue-generating sports, will spend large sums of money on recruiting while other programs do not spend much on recruiting. College recruiting is a complex and challenging process. Given the large number of NCAA academic standards, recruiting guidelines, and stringent timelines, it's no surprise that students and parents are often confused and overwhelmed by how to navigate the process.

While there are no specific formulas to gaining a college athletic scholarship, there are some things that high school student athletes should keep in mind. Many things contribute to a coach deciding to offer a scholarship, but it is universal that most coaches look for talent, abilities, morality, and sportsmanship when recruiting potential athletes to join their teams. Certain behaviors may get students noticed for the wrong reasons. No matter how great a student athlete's athletic prowess is on and off the field or court, there are behaviors that can cool a coach who has been on the recruiting trail. Some student athletes make crucial mistakes in the recruiting process that hinder receiving a college athletic scholarship. There are timelines and deadlines depending on the sport in which a student athlete participates. An athletic scholarship is a means to obtain an education and ultimately receive an undergraduate degree. There is more to college athletics than the competition that people see on television, and there is more to becoming a college athlete than working out, staying in shape, and competing. Being a student athlete means balancing both athletics and academics because, as a student athlete, there is not one without the other.

To help students avoid the pitfalls, the authors have compiled beneficial information to introduce high school and college student athletes to challenges they may face in pursuing a scholarship. We also endeavor to show the importance of a college education and how to pursue a college degree. This guide is practical and particularly suitable for those who seek to enhance their understanding of the intercollegiate scholarship process. As one navigates through this material, they will discover that Part I introduces high school student athletes to a discussion about amateurism vs. professionalism and the history of student athletes and the NCAA. Part I also introduces readers to NCAA-sponsored fall sports, winter sports, and spring sports. Part II discusses how high school students can raise their visibility to get noticed by college recruiters. Part III explains the recruiting process and how to write letters of interest. This section also discusses official and unofficial visits and suggests questions student athletes and their parents should ask college coaches and recruiters. Part IV examines the ins and outs of a college scholarship and navigating NCAA policies and procedures. It also discusses sexual violence and student athletes and adjusting to college life and collegiate athletic competition. Part V reviews habits that support successful academic habits. This section also highlights opportunities after college athletics are over. In Part VI, former college student athletes discuss their experiences as college athletes and life after college athletics.

PART I

Student Athletes and Collegiate Athletics

STUDENT ATHLETE

A student athlete is a participant in an organized competitive sport sponsored by a university or college in which he or she is enrolled. The term *student athlete* implies that for all enrolled college students who participate in sports, the pursuit of education comes first, and sports are secondary, extracurricular activities. The term is used to describe being a full-time student and a full-time athlete, and the balance between the enormous amounts of time engaged in both. In the United States, athletic scholarships are largely regulated by either the National Association of Intercollegiate Athletics (NAIA) or the National Collegiate Athletic Association (NCAA), which sets minimum standards for both the individuals awarded the scholarships and for the member institutions granting scholarships. However, in many cases for some student athletes, time on the practice fields tends to exceed the time spent on academic endeavors. What is the origin of this term *student athlete*? The term surfaced when individuals began to push for college athletes to receive compensation. As a result, to thwart the push to pay college athletes, the term *student athlete* was created by Walter Byers, the first executive director of the NCAA, to disavow attempts to require universities to pay workers' compensation to student athletes.

Prospective Student Athlete

According to the National Collegiate Athletic Association,

A prospective student athlete is a student who has started classes for the ninth grade. In addition, a student who has not started classes for the ninth grade becomes a prospective student athlete if the institution provides such an individual (or the individual's relatives or friends) any financial assistance or other benefits that the institution does not provide to prospective students generally. An individual remains a prospective student athlete until one of the following occurs, (whichever is earlier):

(a) The individual officially registers and enrolls in a minimum full-time program of studies and attends classes in any term of a four-year collegiate institution's regular academic year (excluding summer);

(b) The individual participates in a regular squad practice or competition at a four-year collegiate institution that occurs before the beginning of any term; *(Revised: 1/11/89, 1/10/90, 1/19/13 effective 8/1/13)*;

(c) The individual officially registers, enrolls and attends classes during the certifying institution's summer term prior to his or her initial full-time enrollment at the certifying institution; or *(Adopted: 4/28/05, Revised: 1/17/09, 1/19/13 effective 8/1/13)*;

(d) The individual reports to an institutional orientation session that is open to all incoming students within 14 calendar days prior to the opening day of classes of a regular academic year term. *(Adopted: 1/19/13 effective 8/1/13)*.

AMATEURISM vs. PROFESSIONAL STATUS

Amateur sports are when the athletes participate without getting paid for participating. Professional athletes get paid for playing their sport. The NCAA requires all college athletes to be amateurs and have implemented rules and policies to ensure that athletes who compete in NCAA-sponsored events are amateurs. They also require all incoming student athletes be certified as amateur athletes. With the globalization of college athletics, this is becoming increasingly difficult. To be eligible and to remain eligible to compete, student athletes must not enter into contracts with professional teams or sports clubs, earn a salary for participating in a sport, accept prize money over necessary expenses, compete with professional athletes, try out or practice with a professional team or sports club, hire the services of an agent or a prospective agent, enter into agreement with an agent, or enter initial full-time collegiate enrollment to compete in an organized sports event. The NCAA provides policies on amateurism on its Eligibility Center's Web site. The NCAA began the process of certifying student athletes in 2007. Prior to 2007, each college or university was responsible for ensuring the amateurism of their student athletes. Some student athletes may be declared ineligible or ineligible with conditions. If a student athlete is declared ineligible, that means they cannot compete in any Division I or II sports. A student athlete's amateur status can also be placed under review. If the athlete is placed under review status, this means that an investigation must take place to determine if the student athlete is an amateur or not.

ORIGIN OF THE NCAA, DIFFERENT DIVISION LEVELS, AND OTHER GOVERNING ATHLETIC ASSOCIATIONS

The National Collegiate Athletic Association (NCAA) is the governing body of 23 sports at three different levels of competitions. The NCAA was established in 1906 under another name, Intercollegiate Athletic Association of the United

States. The new name would be adopted in 1910. It is headquartered in Indianapolis, Indiana. The NCCA also sponsors athletic championships, and they oversee the financial operations of college athletics and enforce the rules, policy, and procedures. The NCAA also governs eligibility and promotes sportsmanship and fair competitions. The competition levels are classified as Division I, Division II, and Division III. As of 2016, there were 346 Division I members, 291 Division II members, and 439 Division III members. Any school that participates in collegiate athletics will be classified in one of these divisions. Each university decides in which level of competition they will compete. Many universities take into account their enrollment, financial strength, and fan base, along with the support of their alumni and fans when determining the level they will be classified as. In determining their level of competition, these universities also take into account the number of sports a school offers overall, how many sports are offered for men and women, how many teams the university sponsors and athletes it has for each sport, and the number of athletic competitions it has against schools in the same division. These universities must also take the aforementioned into account when deciding what division level to compete. After universities determine in which level they will compete, they must annually meet the requirements of that particular division.

NCAA Division I level is usually considered to be the top level of competition. These universities' athletic programs are heavily funded and are household names. This division is usually populated with athletes who could possibly become professional athletes. Division I universities must offer at least seven different sports for both men and women. If they cannot equally offer seven different sports for both men and women, they are allowed to offer eight sports for women and six for men and be allowed to retain their Division I status. Division I schools must also offer two team sports for each gender and have both male and female teams and participants for each competitive sport's season. Division I schools must also offer financial aid to their student athletes without going over the maximum amount allowed. Division I universities must also compete in the minimum number of contests against other Division I universities, and this may vary depending on the sport. There are also attendance requirements in football and basketball that Division I schools must meet to remain classified at this level. Division I schools must average 15,000 people in actual or paid attendance per home game. Coaches from Division I schools usually begin recruiting early and expect the student athlete to have participated in high school sports or some other form of amateur or club sports. These coaches usually expect the athletes to be top athletes and also have a good work ethic and attitude.

Universities who compete at the Division II level also meet specific requirements to maintain their classification. Division II is not as driven by money as Division I. Division II coaches appear to have a commitment to coaching their sport and educating the athletes. Division II schools are required to offer a minimum of five sports for men and five for women. If they cannot meet this requirement, they can offer six for women and four for men. In addition, Division II schools must offer two sports for each gender and have both male and female teams participating for each sport during its season. They also must have at least the minimum number of competitions and participants for each sport. Division II athletes receive scholarships. Typically Division II are smaller than Division I institutions. These universities and colleges usually do not have the same financial resources as Division I schools, and therefore, may be constrained giving scholarships. Division II universities usually give partial scholarships to student athletes. The student athletes supplement the portion of their tuition and fees through federal financial aid, student loans, or paying out of pocket. There are 312 Division II universities and colleges in the United States. They are a mixture of public and private and they usually have fewer than 10,000 students enrolled.

Most of America's colleges and universities that offer sports are classified as Division III. Like Division II universities, Division III universities are required to offer a minimum of five sports for men and five for women. Division III schools must also offer two team sports for each gender and have male and female teams or participants for each sports season. At Division III universities, student athletes typically do not receive athletic scholarships. Student athletes who compete at Division III institutions are usually high-achieving academic students. Division III student athletes can balance rigorous academics and competitive athletics. Division III student athletes must meet the same admissions standards and academic standards as the general student body of their university. Division III student athletes do not have the obligation of an athletic scholarship. If a student athlete understands that a professional athletic career is not likely to be in their future, a college education from a Division III institution can be a passport to a great future after college. The Division III level of competition places primary emphasis on regional in-season and conference competition. There are 36 national championship teams annually crowned in this division. Various sports offer competitions at varied times and seasons during the academic year. The NCAA sponsors fall, winter, and spring sports.

Fall Sponsored Sports

Men's and Women's Cross Country

Field Hockey

Football

Men's and Women's Soccer

Women's Volleyball

Men's Water Polo

Winter Sponsored Sports

Men's and Women's Basketball

Bowling

Fencing

Men's and Women's Gymnastics

Men's and Women's Ice Hockey

Men's and Women's Mixed Rifle

Men's and Women's Mixed Skiing

Men's and Women's Swimming and Diving

Men's and Women's Indoor Track and Field

Wrestling

Spring Sponsored Sports

Baseball and Softball

Men's and Women's Golf

Men's and Women's Lacrosse

Rowing

Men's and Women's Tennis

Men's and Women's Outdoor Track and Field

Women's Water Polo

The NCAA also plays a role in recruitment. Student athletes who desire to participate in college athletics must register with the NCAA's Eligibility Center. Student athletes should get assistance navigating the NCAA's system from their coaches, parents, or guardians. They must first create an account on the NCCA Web site and complete registration. Most important, high school student athletes must meet eligibility requirements by completing certain courses during high school and taking the American College Test (ACT) or Scholastic Aptitude Test (SAT) test. While the NCAA is the most noted governing body of college athletics, there are other governing bodies that sanction college athletics.

NATIONAL ASSOCIATION OF INTERCOLLEGIATE ATHLETICS (NAIA)

The National Association of Intercollegiate Athletics (NAIA) headquarters are located in Kansas City, Missouri. This organization is the governing association of small athletics programs that are dedicated to character-driven intercollegiate athletics. The NAIA was founded in 1937, and the organization has provided administrative oversight for college athletics by sponsoring championships. The NAIA attempts to distinguish itself by focusing on the athlete's holistic college educational experience by attempting to make the student athlete the center of the collegiate athletic experience. It is estimated that more than 60,000 student athletes have the opportunity to play college sports at NAIA member institutions each year. The NAIA was the first collegiate athletics association to invite historically black institutions into membership and the first to sponsor both men's and women's national championships. The NAIA sponsors 23 championships and more than 250 colleges and universities compete under its administration. The NAIA also has 21 conferences that are affiliated with its organization. It is estimated that NAIA-affiliated schools award approximately $500 million in athletic scholarships to student athletes. The NAIA sponsors the following sports:

Men's NAIA Fall Sponsored Sports

Cross Country

Football

Soccer

Volleyball

Men's NAIA Winter Sponsored Sports

Basketball Division I and II

Indoor Track and Field

Swimming and Diving

Wrestling

Men's NAIA Spring Sponsored Sports

Baseball

Golf

Outdoor Track and Field

Tennis

Women's NAIA Fall Sponsored Sports

Cross Country

Soccer

Volleyball

Women's NAIA Winter Sponsored Sports

Basketball Division I and II

Indoor Track and Field

Swimming and Diving

Women's NAIA Spring Sponsored Sports

Golf

Outdoor Track and Field

Softball

Tennis

Invitational

Competitive Dance and Cheer

Men and Women's Lacrosse

Men's Volleyball

UNITED STATES COLLEGIATE ATHLETIC ASSOCIATION (USCAA)

The United States Collegiate Athletic Association (USCAA) is another governing body of collegiate athletics that "exists to provide quality athletic competition on a regional and national level. The USCAA focuses specifically on smaller institutions of higher learning and their student athletes. The association believes that all athletes and programs deserve the same national opportunities as larger institutions." The primary goal of the USCAA is to provide members with an association that is devoted to the growth, vision, and values of their institutions. The USCAA has established eligibility and compliance policies and procedures. Most of these policies are similar to the policies established by other governing organizations. The USCAA caters to small colleges with similar resources and allows them to compete for national championships. The USCAA headquarters are located in Newport News, Virginia. Universities who are members of USCAA can also have a dual affiliation with other collegiate athletic governing organizations. Dual membership provides member universities with opportunities to schedule with other schools. The following are USCAA-recognized sports:

Men's Sports

Golf

Cross Country

Soccer

Basketball

Baseball

Wrestling

Women's Sports

Cross Country

Volleyball

Soccer

Basketball

Softball

The USCAA aims not to compete with the NCAA or NAIA for members, but instead provide more opportunities for competition between affiliate schools.

NATIONAL JUNIOR COLLEGE ATHLETIC ASSOCIATION (NJCAA)

In 1937, several track and field coaches met in Fresno, California, to begin discussions on how they could get permission for their athletes to compete in the championships sponsored by the NCAA. Oliver E. Byrd of San Mateo Junior College led the group to write and send a letter to the NCAA. These coaches organized to file a petition on behalf of 13 California two-year schools' track and field athletes to compete at the NCAA championships, but their petition was rejected. Afterward the coaches organized the West Coast Relays and began working on a constitution that would govern their new organization. In 1938, the first constitution of the National Junior College Athletic Association (NJCAA) was ratified, and one year later the organization sponsored its first championships hosted by Sacramento Junior College in 1939. Byrd was elected as the NCJAA's first president. The mission of the NJCAA is to "foster a national program of athletic participation in an environment that supports equitable opportunities" consistent with the educational objectives of its members and promote and foster two-year college athletics. The NCJAA has expanded since its inception and sponsors all of the following sports.

Men's Sports

Basketball

Bowling

Cross Country

Football

Golf

Half Marathon

Ice Hockey

Lacrosse

Soccer

Swimming and Diving

Tennis

Track and Field

Wrestling

Women's Sports

Basketball

Bowling

Cross Country

Golf

Half Marathon

Lacrosse

Soccer

Swimming and Diving

Tennis

Track and Field

The NCJAA's national headquarters are located in Colorado Springs, Colorado. The NCJAA has over 500 member schools across the United States. Each year almost 60,000 student athletes compete in the 23 sports that the organization sponsors. Like the NCAA, at the conclusion of each sport season teams from across the nation compete for national championships sponsored by the NCJAA. There have been a number of student athletes who have participated through events sponsored by the NCJAA, notably the first high school player to go straight to the NBA, Spencer Haywood (Trinidad State Junior College); Heisman Trophy winner and NFL Hall of Famer Roger Stabauch (New Mexico Military Institute); the first African American to play at the University of Alabama, John Mitchell (Eastern Arizona College); the NBA player Anthony "Spud" Webb (Midland College); Major League Baseball star Jim Thome (Illinois Central College); Women National Basketball Association legend Sheryl Swoopes (South Plains College); Softball legend Crystl Butos (Palm Beach Community College); Major League Baseball's Albert Pujols (Maple Woods Community College); Heisman Trophy Winner and NFL quarterback Cam Newton (Blinn Community College); Major League Baseball star Bryce Harper (College of Southern Nevada); and Super Bowl winner and NFL cornerback Malcom Butler (Hinds Junior College). Junior college may be the route for some student athletes to show their talent, skills, and abilities for a Division I or Division II university.

HISTORY OF ATHLETIC SCHOLARSHIPS IN COLLEGIATE SPORTS

During the early 1800s when schools began to compete against each other, athletic scholarships were not a part of the equation. The idea of athletic scholarships for college athletes began when the University of Chicago's football coach Amos

Alonzo Stagg began to provide student service payments. As a result of these service payments the University of Chicago grew into a national powerhouse in football, which brought large financial resources to the university. This became the model for other universities, and big-time college athletics and higher education have become inseparable. While the University of Chicago introduced the concept of athletic scholarships, initially they were intended for males only. After the initial offering of scholarships, this initiative of providing scholarships for athletics began to be abused. During the 1950s, large schools began handing out as many athletic scholarships as they could. In some cases, scholarships were given just to prevent student athletes from attending their competitors, especially in the sports of basketball and football. It was not uncommon for some schools to have 150 players on a football team and as many as 25 players on a basketball team through the 1960s. Athletic scholarship for females did not take shape until the 1970s. All student athletes have heard of the notion of full-ride scholarships. For the most part, this is a myth. Scholarships are initially for only one year and are renewable on a year-to-year basis. The decision on whether a scholarship will be renewed is usually left up to the head coach. In addition, scholarships are actually called "grants-in-aid" and apply only to Division I-A and I-AA schools. Division III schools do not offer athletic scholarships. In the 1970s, the NCAA imposed a limit of 105 scholarships for football programs. This decision along with the passage of federal Title IX legislation forced universities to allocate money for women's sports. Throughout the years, a reduction of football scholarships continued from 95 in 1978 to 85 in 1992. Currently, Division I Football Bowl Series universities and Division I AA Football Championship Series universities are allowed only 63 scholarships in football. In an effort to ensure collegiate sports remain equitable, there are measures in place. Among identical Division I-A sports, women have more athletic scholarships available than men in softball/baseball, fencing, cross country, track and field, golf, gymnastics, skiing, soccer, swimming, tennis, volleyball, and water polo. Lacrosse is the only sport that is offered for both men and women where there are more men's scholarships offered. Women are offered six more sports than men, and this trend is almost the same in Division I-AA athletic programs.

WHAT IT TAKES TO GET RECRUITED IN COLLEGIATE ATHLETICS

High school student athletes often ask the question, "What does it take to get a college athletic scholarship?" Coaches are interested in student athletes who possess a great talent and athletic abilities but who also have strong grade point averages and good standard test scores. All athletes need to play at a high level in high school to gain the attention of coaches. College coaches want good players. Coaches hope to recruit players who will give them the best opportunities to win and keep their jobs. When high schools are fortunate to have several good student athletes, it means that the high school will receive a lot of attention from college recruiters. If a high school has proven itself to be a producer of great collegiate talent, then this will help high school athletes. If the high school is not accustomed to handle the recruiting process, this may also hinder high school athletes being recruited. If a high school has a relationship with particular colleges, coaches usually attempt to steer athletes to those universities. A student's high school coach's recommendation is important. If the student's high school coach provides a bad report to a recruiter, the recruiting university may lose interest in recruiting them. Reports such as having a poor work ethic or difficult to coach can hinder students from receiving scholarship offers. Sometimes coaches are not completely honest in assessing a student athlete's abilities because they want to avoid potential conflict. There are several reasons why a high school student athlete may not be getting recruited. The most obvious reason is that the student athlete may not have enough talent to play at the collegiate level. If a student believes he or she is good enough to play on the college level, the student should research potential schools and send them a highlight video, recruiting profile, and a letter. Students should keep track of coaches and athletic departments that respond. For those who do respond, students should send a follow up within about two to three weeks after the initial contact. Unless a student is a blue-chip athlete (high level players who are already targeted for recruitment), there is no perfect path to getting recruiting.

INITIAL ELIGIBILITY FOR DIVISION I AND DIVISION II ATHLETICS

To be eligible to compete in college athletics, high school student athletes must meet specific requirements. To remain eligible while a college athlete, there are requirements that also must be met. Student athletes attempting to become eligible for college athletics must satisfactorily complete 16 core courses in high school and have an acceptable score on the ACT or SAT. Scores on these standardized examinations are used on a sliding scale and balanced with the high school grade point average of the college athlete to determine eligibility.

The NCAA offers an Eligibility Center on its Web site at http://www.ncaa.org /student-athletes/future/eligibility-center. To be eligible and a full qualifier to compete in Division I athletics, student athletes are required to complete 16 core courses. These courses include four years of English course work, plus three years of math that includes Algebra I or higher. The student athlete must also complete two years of natural or physical science. The science requirement may be reduced to one year if there is a lab associated with the science course. To be eligible, student athletes must also take two years of social science and four years of additional course work in math, science, social science, or any foreign language or comparative religion/philosophy course. In addition to the English, math, and science requirements mentioned above, a student athlete must also take one additional English, math, or science course to become eligible to compete in college athletics at the Division I level.

To be eligible to compete in college sports sanctioned by the NCAA, student athletes must be placed on an active Institutional Request List (IRL). Student athletes must register on the NCAA Eligibility Center's online site. There is a $50 fee associated with this process. Students must complete an online form and have their high school transcript sent to the NCAA. After completing the online registration, the student must request that a college coach place his or her name on the IRL list. The coach will contact the NCAA and ask that the information and application be cleared by the NCAA clearinghouse. Once one coach requests that a student be cleared and clearance has been granted, then he or she will be eligible to play at any NCAA-sanctioned school. To be cleared, the student athlete must have a grade point average of 2.0, an SAT score of 810, or an ACT score of 18. A graduated scale is used and the higher the student athlete's grade point average, the lower the standardized test score may be. The NCAA's "sliding scale" allows a higher core grade point average to reduce the SAT component. A 2.5 core grade point average will need a 820 SAT score, a higher core grade point average of 2.75 will need a 720 SAT score, a 3.0 core GPA will only require a 620 SAT score and a 3.55 core grade point average will just need a 400 SAT score. The NCAA has stated that their research now indicates that core class grades were the best indicators of academic success during a student athlete's freshman year. The student must also be admitted to the university in which they will participate in athletics. Due to the huge number of eligibility applications of potential student athletes' submissions to the NCAA Eligibility Center, this process can take as long as six to eight months to complete. If students are delayed in making requests, their eligibility approval can be postponed. In some instances, high school players who have procrastinated in completing the clearinghouse registration have lost out on admissions to the university they chose to accept a scholarship. It is prudent that student athletes complete their application as soon as possible and become eligible.

HEAD COUNT SPORTS

The sanctioned sports in the NCAA are divided into two categories, head count sports and equivalency sports. Head count sports have a set number of scholarships that can be offered, and the number of athletes receiving awards cannot exceed that number, so these sports usually only offer full scholarships. They are generally revenue-generating sports, and there are only six head count sports at the Division I level: football (Football Bowl Subdivision only), men's and women's basketball, women's volleyball, women's tennis, and women's gymnastics. The competition for scholarships in these sports is very high, and they are typically given to the most elite athletes in a given sport. Equivalency sports also have a set number of scholarships, but they can be divided among multiple athletes. Some athletes may receive a full scholarship, while others receive a portion of a scholarship. However, there is still a limit on the number of athletes who are allowed to receive even a partial scholarship, known as *counters*. Equivalency sports are typically nonrevenue sports, and while the competition for scholarships is still high, there is a better chance of earning a partial scholarship. The equivalency men's Division I sports are baseball, rifle, skiing, cross country, track and field, soccer, fencing, swimming, golf, tennis, gymnastics, volleyball, ice hockey, water polo, lacrosse, and wrestling. On the women's side, the head count sports for Division I are basketball, gymnastics, tennis, and volleyball. The equivalency sports in women's Division I are bowling, lacrosse, rowing, cross country, track and field, skiing, fencing, soccer, field hockey, softball, golf, swimming, ice hockey, and water polo. All of Division II and NAIA programs are equivalency sports.

SUGGESTED READINGS

Adler, Peter, and Patricia A. Adler. "Role Conflict and Identity Salience: College Athletics and the Academic Role." *Social Science Journal* 24, no. 4 (1987): 443–455.

Brake, Deborah L. *Getting in the Game: Title IX and the Women's Sports Revolution.* New York: New York University Press, 2010.

Byers, Walter. *Unsportsmanlike Conduct: Exploiting College Athletes.* Ann Arbor: University of Michigan Press, 2010.

Comeaux, Eddie. *Introduction to Intercollegiate Athletics.* Baltimore: Johns Hopkins University Press, 2015.

Duquin, Mary. "Sport and Emotions." In *Handbook of Sports Studies*, edited by Jay Coakley and Eric Dunning, 477– 489. London: Sage, 2000.

Gerdy, John R. *Air Ball: American Education's Failed Experiment with Elite Athletics.* Jackson: University Press of Mississippi, 2006.

Lapchick, Richard E. *New Game Plan for College Sport.* Santa Barbara, CA: Greenwood, 2006.

National Collegiate Athletic Association. http://www.gomason.com/fls/25200/data _import/photos/sports/genrel/auto_pdf/09-10-div1-manual.pdf?DB_OEM _ID=25200.

National Collegiate Athletic Association. "Cost of Attendance Q&A." http:// www.ncaa.com/news/ncaa/article/2015–09–03/cost-attendance-qa.

Nixon, Howard L. *The Athletic Trap: How College Sports Corrupted the Academy.* Baltimore: Johns Hopkins University Press, 2014.

PART II

Getting Noticed as a High School Student Athlete

STEP ONE: PREPARING FOR COLLEGIATE ATHLETICS

General Recruiting Process

The general process for recruiting involves a series of steps that coaches will employ at various points. The first step requires generating initial interest through letters, questionnaires, and camp invites. During this step, coaches are looking to fill the recruiting class with top talent, including targeting generic numbers for height, weight, sport rankings, and personal statistics. The initial letters and other materials that are sent out are used to create a database of athletes and their contact information. Step two involves coaches making initial evaluations, through watching highlight film, looking at times, and talking to high school coaches about training. The objective of this step is to attempt to determine the potential of the athletes in the recruiting pool. Once the list of recruits has been narrowed, coaches will perform secondary evaluations by contacting the family of a recruit and hosting visits. This step (step three) is the beginning of the advanced recruiting interest, where coaches will watch the athletes in person and actively make calls for official and unofficial visits.

Coaches continue to evaluate everything about the athlete, such as character, athletic ability, and academic success. While this is typically understood as a sign of genuine interest, it does not guarantee a scholarship offer. Step four occurs when an offer is extended and a commitment is secured from a recruited athlete. Coaches will meet, rank recruits, and extend offers (scholarship or walk-on) after the evaluation period. These offers will often be accompanied by a time limit, which asks the recruit to make a commitment in a matter of weeks or days after the offer is made. In some cases, programs will be willing to hold a scholarship offer for an undisputed number one recruit. Coaches will continue to evaluate recruits until they are able to reach the fifth step, signing the recruited athletes.

Athletes must still be conscious that nothing is official until they have signed, as a scholarship is not guaranteed by a verbal commitment. A scholarship may still be rescinded for various reasons, including coaching changes, a decline in grades, injury to the recruited athlete, and getting in trouble on social media. The sixth, and final, step in the recruiting process is signing the National Letter of Intent (NLI). Signing the NLI marks the end of the recruiting process, and establishes an agreement that the athlete will enroll in a certain school in exchange for athletic aid. Once the NLI has been signed, other coaches have to cease contact, and athletes must tell them they have signed the NLI.

An NLI is a document that certifies that a student athlete is guaranteed an athletic scholarship for one year by the university that has recruited them. If a student is being recruited by multiple athletic programs, once he or she signs a letter of intent, all other universities must discontinue recruiting that student. A letter of intent is a binding contract, but it is binding for only one academic year. The NLI does not guarantee a student athlete a starting position, playing time, or even a spot on the team. It is merely an agreement that the student athlete agrees to attend the university for one year and the school agrees to pay all or part of their tuition and fees for one year. If the student athlete is under age 21, a parent or guardian must also sign the letter of intent, and it will include an official scholarship. College coaches are prohibited from attending the signing or any staged signing event. Each sport has specific signing periods and all sports have an early signing period that runs for exactly one week. It runs from the second Wednesday in November to the following Wednesday. Below are the general signing periods for collegiate sports, as defined by College Sports Scholarships (http://www.collegesportsscholarships.com/):

- **All Sports Including Basketball**: The early signing period for all sports including basketball begins on the second Wednesday of November lasting one week, thus ending on the following Wednesday.
- **Football Midyear Junior College Transfer**: The identified signing period for football student athletes seeking midyear transfer from a junior college begins on the third Wednesday in December through January 15th.
- **Football in General**: The signing period opens on the first Wednesday in February, concluding on April 1.
- **Basketball**: The signing period opens on the second Wednesday in April, ending on the third Wednesday in May.
- **Field Hockey, Track and Field, Soccer, Men's Water Polo, Cross Country**: There is no identified early signing period for these sports. The regular signing period begins on the first Wednesday in February and concludes on August 1.
- **All Other Sports**: Regular signing period for any sport/s not previously addressed begins on the second Wednesday in April, concluding on August 1.

Student athletes must wait until 7:00 a.m. of the first day of the signing period to sign the letter of intent. Student athletes and their parents should have a full understanding of the letter of intent.

General Recruiting Tips

Student athletes seeking to get noticed by athletic programs should construct a recruiting profile report. In this profile report, the student athlete should list their significant statistics. There is essential information that should be included in the profile report. This information should include the student athlete's address, phone number, and e-mail addresses. If the coach agrees, include the coach's contact information also. The profile report should also include information about the student athlete's grades and other academic information. Provide your grade point average, and if the ACT or SAT has been taken, provide the score. Class ranking may also be listed, if it can be obtained. The more information that can be provided in the profile, the more the chances improve of obtaining an athletic scholarship offer. Provide game statistics in the profile and this information should be truthful information. If a student is a multiple-sport athlete, any statistics from other sports or accomplishments should be added to the profile. This enhances the profile and adds an added dimension to the profile report. The profile report should also have at least one photograph of the student athlete but multiple photos (two at the most) may be better. An action shot for one photo and a head shot for the other should be sufficient.

Market Yourself and Make a Highlight Tape

High school athletes wishing to get noticed and ultimately get a scholarship to continue competing in college athletics should make a highlight video. Highlight videos are not the sole determinant of whether student athletes get a scholarship, but it can help them get attention from a few schools that may not be aware of their talent. Only the best players in the nation get scholarship offers based on a highlight video, but it may be the difference in a coach deciding whether to consider pursuing a student athlete. The highlight video should consist of about 20 to 30 plays and should be about five minutes long. The highlights should be exceptional plays that showcase the student athlete's ability. Coaches view a lot of highlight tapes, and any video over five minutes may be discarded. It is important to make sure that the video is of high quality. The student athlete's coach may provide quality competition or game video that can be used in the highlight video. Some people hire a professional videographer to shoot footage and edit the highlight tape to ensure that it is of excellent quality. Providing a good-quality highlight video makes it easier for coaches to assess talent and make better evaluations. If coaches like what they see, they may make a request to see an entire game or competition. Because a highlight video only shows spectacular plays, a coach may want to see other aspects of the student athlete's leadership qualities and how they engage in competition when the action is not coming their way. A full game or competition video can show a coach the student athlete's effort, ability, and attitude during competition.

Student athletes should put vital information in their videos such as home phone number, cell phone number, e-mail address, and home address. Jersey number and other measurables such as height, weight, bench and squat stats, and speed should be included in the highlight video. Do not go overboard with the special effects when constructing the video because this could be distracting to viewers.

The video should have some music in the background. Copyrighted music should not be used, and upbeat music without lyrics work best. Student athletes may mail coaches a copy of the highlight DVD and should post the video on Web sites and through social media. The video may also be shared with coaches, family, and friends. This expands the student athlete's network and exposure.

Quick Tips on Creating an Excellent Highlight Video

- Keep the video short. In most cases, coaches usually do not watch the entire video, so keep it short.
- Put best plays at the beginning of the video. This helps get coaches' attention quickly.
- Show various skills. This allows coaches to see a student athlete's versatility.
- The video must be good quality. This shows an investment in the recruitment process.

The highlight video must convey the student athlete's skill. If the student athlete plays several positions in a sport, it may be best to include highlights for several different positions.

STEP TWO: PERFORMING AT AN OPTIMAL LEVEL IN THE CLASSROOM AND IN THE SPORTS ARENA

Study Skills and Good Study Habits

It is important to be willing to prepare your mind to be ready for college. Writing essays and taking tests is much more challenging in college. Good note-taking skills will translate to performing well in college and will simplify the process of studying for exams by removing the stress of being unprepared. College homework will consist of more substantial amounts of reading and writing. Doing work outside the classroom on assignments and other materials for a class will be just as crucial as the work done in the actual classroom. While it is important to develop your own style of studying and managing your time and work, students may want to consider what time of the day they work best and are the most alert. Student athletes must identify the times of the day when their energy levels are at their highest; this is the optimal time to attempt to complete assignments and term papers. If a student works best in the morning, they should not plan all of their study time for the evening. On occasion, it can be okay to still do work at the last minute, but this is not a good habit for a successful college student athlete to form. It is a good idea to have a special space and time where a student knows he or she can be productive studying. It is very important to schedule study time and determine a special place to study.

Student athletes should also optimize their work environment by making sure that their physical environment is conducive to concentration and studying and free from distractions. Student athletes should also guard their time by blocking off periods of time that are dedicated for studying. This may require students to say no to various activities, and people requesting services or attention. To avoid interruptions while studying, students may arrange their work area and sit with their backs to the traffic flow of the study area. Students could also simply close the door to the area where they are studying and not respond to any visitor that may knock on the door. Students may also find it useful to find and use a special space such as a library carrel or an office where others will be unable to locate them. Students should also turn off their cell phones while studying and listen to messages or return missed calls during a study break. During the period that is blocked off for studying, students must STUDY. Do school work and refrain from checking e-mail, checking Facebook, watching television, and surfing the Internet. Students should also take their school work with them. Students can incorporate studying into their daily routines by taking work with them and studying while waiting for the events to start, riding the bus, or during downtime at work. They can use flash cards or begin work on assignments in between breaks and other spare moments at work.

ACT and SAT Exams and High School Grade Point Average

In the United States, there are two exams that colleges and universities use to measure students' aptitude and learning. The Scholastic Aptitude Test (SAT) and the American College Test (ACT) are exams that most schools use to determine, or as a part of a formula on, admission decisions. The ACT is an achievement test that measures what a student has learned. The SAT is more of an aptitude test or reasoning and verbal abilities. The ACT has five components: English, Math, Reading, Science, and an optional writing portion. The SAT has three components that include Critical Reasoning, Mathematics, and a writing test (made optional in 2014). The ACT has about 200 questions plus the optional essay, while the SAT has 170 questions. Students taking the SAT find that the questions get more difficult as the test progresses, while the ACT maintains a constant level of difficulty. The SAT has more emphasis on verbal skills, and students who will take the SAT should build their vocabularies. Both exams are multiple choice tests; however, on the SAT some math questions will have to be worked out by hand. Both exams take approximately three hours and thirty minutes. Students are allowed breaks while taking both tests.

One of the major differences between the ACT and the SAT is the science portion of the test that is given on the ACT. On the ACT, there are questions from biology, chemistry, physics, and earth science. This portion of the test is accessing a student's ability to understand graphs, research summaries, and understand hypotheses. While having taken some of these science courses would be helpful and probably boost a student's score on the ACT science portion, if a student has strong critical reading skills, they can determine the correct answers. The ACT also has questions in trigonometry, while the SAT does not. Students should at least have a basic understanding of trigonometry. One of the major differences between the ACT and SAT is that the SAT penalizes students random guessing. The ACT has no guessing penalty. This does not make one exam better or easier than the other—simply that being knowledgeable about this penalty may assist in not being penalized for hapless guessing. The scoring scales for the two exams are different. Each section of the ACT is out of 36 points, while on the SAT each section is out of 800 points. While it is difficult to get a perfect score, on both students are encouraged to do their best because most colleges and universities in the United States have come to rely on the scores on these tests in admission decisions. As defined by collegeboard.org, the SAT has three sections: Critical Reading, Mathematics, and Writing. Each section of the SAT is scored on a scale from 200 to 800, which means a 2,400 would be a perfect score. The average score of most students is about 500 for each section, with an average total score near 1,500. The ACT consists of four parts: English Language, Reading, Mathematics, and Science. The individual categories are all scored from 1 to 36, with 1 being the lowest possible score and 36 being the highest. The scores from each category are then averaged to determine the composite score. The average composite score is around 21. In 2016, the SAT will return to a 1,600 point scale and eliminate antiquated vocabulary words. Other changes to the SAT consist of the Essay section becoming optional. In addition, the test will no longer penalize students for wrong answers, and the Reading Comprehension section will incorporate subjects that students typically learn in high school. Below are a few strategies to assist students in maximizing preparation before taking the SAT or ACT.

- Students should familiarize themselves with all parts of the exam because this improves their confidence. Students should be familiar with all parts of the exam.
- Students should study unfamiliar vocabulary. Being familiar with words can increase their overall score. Vocabulary is associated with reasoning and critical thinking. Students and their tutors should create flashcards to aid in remembering words and their usages.
- Students should review math consistently. Reviewing math and the processes of working out several math problems will allow students to focus on mathematical knowledge that is key to solving math problems.
- Students should take practice exams. If possible, students should enroll in a preparation course or at the least buy a study guide book and take the practice exams at the conclusion of the book.
- Students should examine incorrect answers. There is a lot of information that can be gained by studying the answers that they got wrong on the practice study exams. This also prevents students from making the same kinds of mistakes when they take the real ACT or SAT.

These standardized tests are not necessarily the best measurement of college success. These exams do not measure intelligence. When these exams became the norm around the mid-1920s, "aptitude" was a code word for intelligence. Students whose family income is high usually score higher on these types of tests. These tests do not measure students' determination and grit in the pursuit of their college education. Student athletes should pick the exam that best accentuates their individual strengths. If a school prefers one test over another, then the student should prepare for that preferred test. The cost to take either the ACT or SAT is roughly the same price, which is approximately $55.00.

Test scores are critically important and care should be taken about reporting test score results to colleges. Students should not report their test results until after they have obtained the scores they feel are the highest they can achieve. Rather than indicating which colleges to send scores to before they take the test, they should wait until after they receive their scores and then report. Many parents and students do not realize this is a viable option.

The Injured High School Athlete

Injuries to high school athletes occur every year, and while it may lead to a change in plans, an injury does not automatically end a student athlete's chances of playing in college. Most important, an injured athlete should be honest with any coaches they have been in contact with. It may be difficult to admit the injury, but lying could negatively impact the chances of receiving a scholarship. It is also possible that some coaches may stop recruiting an athlete depending on the severity of an injury. An injured student athlete must be conscious of the different responsibilities that are required after an injury is suffered. It is important for the injured student athlete to research colleges that may be interesting and provide a chance to play in the future. Injured student athletes should also send highlight and full-game videos to coaches. In the case that an injury impedes the chances of playing at a four-year school right after high school, there are other options to consider that will allow a student athlete to play in college.

A student athlete who has suffered an injury late in his or her high school career may need to attend a junior college first. This will allow the athlete to play and gain experience at a higher level of competition. It will also serve as a display of the ability to overcome the injury and rehab processes. The student athlete may then transfer from the junior college to a four-year school, provided they meet the transfer requirements. Any time an injury occurs, it is important for a student athlete to remain calm and remember key information during the recovery process. First, the injured athlete should gather all the relevant available information before conveying messages to any coaches. This information includes the specific evaluation from the doctor, the severity of the injury, and a possible recovery time. It is also important to keep coaches informed and updated regarding the diagnosis and prognosis during the injury timeline.

An injured student athlete should prepare for any type of response when discussing their injury with coaches, positive or negative, as each coach will react differently. After gathering the information about an injury, the student athlete must then be sure to properly care for him- or herself. It is important to remain patient and not push the injury to heal too soon. The primary focus should shift to getting healthy and remaining eligible to play in the future. It is also likely for an injured student athlete to experience mental and emotional stress, at which point he or she should find someone to talk to. Finally, any injured student athlete should maintain a positive attitude. Injuries are common, and they require time to heal, but it does not signify the end of the recruiting process.

No Scholarship Offers: Now What

For families who do not have the financial means to pay for college out of pocket, there are options to fund a college education. Scholarships are a great way to pay for college if your family cannot finance your college education. There are more than a million scholarships awarded each year. There are scholarships provided on the basis of academic merit, disability, race, nationality, and religious affiliation. In some cases, scholarships are not awarded because no one applies or those who apply are not eligible for scholarships. The Federal Pell Grant is another way for those who cannot pay for college out of pocket. The grant is awarded to students who have not earned a bachelor's degree. Students can receive up to $5,550 for the award year, for up to 12 semesters. Institutional grants are financial aid that is sponsored by the institution, are merit based, and cover the gap of tuition that is not covered by federal financial aid. Students may also apply for a loan to pay for school. Some of the most popular loans are the Parent PLUS Loan, Federal Perkins, Direct Subsidized, and Direct Unsubsidized loans. Other sources to pay for college include federal work-study programs, military service, and employee assistance.

Student fees are various charges that can range from laboratory fees to parking fees if the student owns a car and intends to park on campus. Universities usually provide a student fee total; however, they may not break down all fees and only itemize the most significant fees. There may be fees for student identification card fees, health insurance fees, gym facility usage fees, athletic activity fees, diplomas and graduation expenses, computer access, local bus service, and student activities. The most common fees assessed are those associated with a lab for a course in which the student is enrolled. There are fees usually associated with science, technology, and engineering courses. Students and parents should contact the registrar's office, campus cashier, or financial aid office to get a better explanation of any charge or fee assessed by a university. Students should examine their student bills and check for fees that may be charged. Students must make sure that any fees have been rightly charged to them.

Finances and Financial Aid

Students may also hear various terms associated with student financial aid. Financial aid is financial assistance students and their families receive in the form of scholarships, grants, work-study, and loans for education. There are many terms used in determining the type of financial aid provided to students. *Merit-based aid* is offered in the form of scholarships and funds that require additional criteria to be met beyond the demonstrations of financial need. All student applicants are eligible, but award decisions are often influenced by several factors, such as academic performance in high school, leadership involvement, or talent. In addition to merit-based aid, schools will offer *need-based aid*, which is financial aid that evaluates financial need as the primary determining factor. Some universities use a *need-blind policy* to determine admissibility of applicants. A need-blind admission policy is when a university does not consider the financial needs of the applicant when determining admissibility. In contrast, a *need-aware policy* is when a college or university does take into consideration the financial needs of the applicant when determining admissibility. Students should consider these policies when making their final decisions about which university to attend.

There are several types of financial aid offered to students who meet certain financial criteria. Grants are financial aid that does not need to be repaid. Grant decisions are based on family income, household size, reported assets, and the number of children in college. To receive aid from federal programs, a student must:

- qualify for financial need (except for certain loans);
- have a high school diploma or a General Education Development (GED) certificate, or pass a test approved by the U.S. Department of Education;
- be working toward a degree or certificate;
- be enrolled in an eligible program;
- be a U.S. citizen or eligible noncitizen;
- have a valid Social Security number; and
- maintain satisfactory academic progress once in school.

The most common grant is the Pell Grant, which pays for tuition, fees, and books, and refunds to the student any unused money. Student loans must be paid back to the lender. If students take out loans to pay for college, they must pay back the lender along with the interest on the debt taken for their college education. Student athletes should know that they have the power and the control over how much money they borrow and spend. They should be fully aware of the responsibility, repayment, and interest rates. Historically the interest rates associated with student loans were fixed, but now these rates are adjustable and could increase depending on federal interest rates. Scholarships do not require repayment. These are the most underused in financial aid categories because each scholarship and its funding agency have established their own criteria for their scholarship. They can be based on academics and various other categories. Many scholarships have been designed specifically for students of color. Most universities will have applications for all internal scholarships. Various civic groups and organizations will offer scholarships, and they should be contacted directly for their scholarship applications and requirements. Work-study is also another common way college students earn money for their educations.

Scholarships are financial aid money awarded. These funds do not have to be repaid. Scholarships are awarded based on numerous factors, such as cultural background, academics, and extracurricular activities. A separate application process is usually required. FAFSA is the Free Application for Federal Student Aid. This application for financial aid is a form that students must fill out to be considered for both state and federal financial aid. This application becomes available in January of each year. The government must receive a student's application before March of each year to be considered for the state portion, and the FAFSA form must be renewed each year. After submitting the forms, the student will receive an award letter in an official letter of notification from a school where the student has been accepted. This letter outlines the student's financial aid award package. Students may finance their college education through loans. Loans are financial aid money available to students and parents. This money has to be repaid. Loan programs may be from the government or from private companies, and the terms and interest rates vary depending on the lending source.

Fellowships are financial awards usually awarded to graduate and postgraduate students. The financial awards usually have requirements associated with receiving them. They may require a student to conduct research under the guidance of a professor or be employed in an office on campus. Fellowships may have a tuition waiver, and they may have an additional stipend associated with them. Grants are financial aid money that does not have to be repaid to their funding sources. Grants are available through many different sources such as the federal government, state agencies, and individual universities. Grants are like scholarships in that they provide students with financial aid that they are not required to repay. The funds are applied to school expenses in the same way student loans are applied. These funds can be used for tuition, books, housing, and other costs associated with postsecondary education.

Walk-on vs. Preferred Walk-on

A "walk-on" is an individual who makes the team, does not receive any athletic scholarship, and yet is still eligible to receive academic aid. Some student athletes may choose to walk-on as a result of coaches allocating all scholarship money for a given year. Walking-on may also be an option for those student athletes who attempt to play at a higher level that does not match their talent, or for student athletes who started the recruiting process too late. In order to walk-on, a student athlete must be diligent in contacting coaches. He or she must also register for the

NCAA Eligibility Center and send official transcripts directly from the high school attended. Walk-on student athletes must also receive a physical medical exam, and they must be enrolled in the school for which they wish to play.

A "preferred walk-on" is similar to a regular walk-on, with some additional advantages. Preferred walk-ons are typically recruited by the coach and have been guaranteed a spot on the team. They are not offered scholarship money as a freshman, but there is a possibility of receiving a scholarship in the future. In some cases, preferred walk-ons maintain a separate status from regular walk-ons, as they may be treated the same as scholarship players. However, a preferred walk-on is still subject to the transfer rules of his or her particular sport.

Junior College Route

Before transferring from a junior college to a four-year institution, a student athlete must enlist the help of both the athletic department from the school they are attending and from the school to which they wish to transfer. Typically, there are two types of junior college transfers: 2–4 transfers and 4–2–4 transfers.

2–4 Transfers

A student athlete attempting to transfer from a junior/community college to a four-year institution is considered to be a 2–4 transfer. There are two levels of being a 2–4 transfer: academic qualifier and nonqualifier. In order to be considered as an academic qualifier, a student athlete must meet certain requirements. First, they must be registered with the NCAA Eligibility Center. Second, they must be certified by the NCAA Eligibility Center as an academic qualifier. Third, the student athlete wishing to transfer must attend the two-year college full-time for at least one semester or quarter. Fourth, the prospective transfer must achieve a minimum GPA of at least 2.000. Finally, the student athlete must complete an average of at least 12 transferrable credit hours per full-time term at the two-year college.

A nonqualifier transfer is a student athlete who is attempting to transfer before completing a general/associate degree. The restrictions for a nonqualifier transfer differ according to whether a student athlete wishes to transfer to a Division I or Division II institution. If a student athlete attempts to transfer to a Division I institution, there are four primary requirements that must be met. First, the student athlete must attend a two-year college full-time for at least three semesters or four quarters. Second, a minimum GPA of 2.000 must be achieved. Third, the student athlete must graduate from the two-year college. Finally, the prospective transfer must have at least 48 transferable credit hours at a semester school or 72 transferable credit hours at a quarter school, including six semester hours or eight quarter hours of English and three semester hours or four quarter hours of math.

A student athlete attempting to transfer to a Division II institution must also meet two specific criteria. First, they must have attended a two-year college for at least two semesters or three quarters. Second, the student athlete must either graduate from the two-year college or complete an average of 12 credit hours for every full-time semester or quarter at the two-year college.

4–2–4 Transfers

A 4–2–4 transfer is a student athlete who has previously attended a four-year school before attending junior college. In order for a student athlete to transfer to a Division I school, they must again meet all the criteria. First, they must complete an average of 12 hours of transferrable degree credit per term of full-time attendance at the junior college. Second, the student athlete must achieve a minimum GPA of at least 2.000. Third, at least one calendar year must elapse since the student athlete left the original four-year school. Finally, the student athlete must graduate from the junior college. The rules for any student athlete wishing to transfer to a Division II school are the same as the 2–4 transfer rules.

Application and Admission to a University

While athletic ability and performance are paramount for any high school or college student athlete, classroom performance is the most important to their athletic career. The application process is the most important factor in getting admitted to any college or university. Each application must be completely filled out. Applicants must take care to check their grammar and spelling, and then have their applications proofread by a parent, teacher, guidance counselor, or someone they trust with the skills and experience to give positive feedback. It is best to fill out applications either online or use downloaded applications. This should be the first option before completing handwritten applications. Before completing the application, read all instructions carefully to ensure understanding of all application requirements and what each line of the application is specifically asking. If more clarity is needed on any item on the application, call the college's admissions office for clarity.

Students should apply to colleges early. In general, students in their junior year of high school should begin the initial stages of considering what universities they may want to attend. This also takes the pressure of making this decision off of the student during their senior year of high school. Early action admission is an accelerated application process where students usually apply in November and receive a college decision by January. This shows that a student is highly interested in the university and is serious about attending the university to which he or she is applying. Early admissions applications also give students a better chance of obtaining financial aid and scholarships. Planning ahead and applying early allows students to have the security of knowing where they are attending and not stress over an admission decision. It also allows students to weigh other offers and possibly bargain for a better financial package from a competing school. Most scholarships are offered on a first come, first serve basis and therefore applying late may limit a student's opportunity to receive a scholarship.

Some universities use a rolling admission process. In a rolling admission process, applicants have a large window of time to apply for admission. Most of the elite schools do not use a rolling process. The process usually opens during the fall and may continue up until the summer. In the rolling process, students are usually notified of the admission decision within a few weeks. Universities that use a rolling admission process typically accept students as long as there are spaces available. An open admission process typically allows any student with a high school diploma or a GED to enroll at the university. In an open enrollment process, students may still have to make a minimum score on the ACT or SAT and have a certain grade point average to gain admittance. The earliest students should start considering college application is 12 to 16 months prior to enrolling in college. Students should write to the universities they have chosen and request application materials, catalogs, and information about financial aid, housing, and fields of study. Students can also get this information on the universities' Web sites. Students should complete their college application in a timely manner and pay attention to prospective colleges' deadlines. These deadlines are listed on the application forms. Colleges and universities receive thousands of applications from students each year. In order to be considered for admission at the college of your choice for the term you want to begin, it is essential that your application and all supporting materials such as references and personal essay be received before the deadline. To have a good beginning at the application process, students should carefully follow the instructions of each school to which they are considering. If students have any questions about the application process, they should call the college's admission office to clarify any questions.

The "common application" can be used by students to apply to institutions in the United States, Austria, France, Germany, Italy, Switzerland, and the United Kingdom. The common application is managed by The Common Application Incorporated, which is a nonprofit organization whose mission is to provide a holistic admission process. This process takes into account both subjective and objective measures by using the applicant's essays, recommendations, standardized testing, and class rank. Even if students do use common applications, most applications are handled electronically. Before an application is submitted, review all the application materials and proofread the personal statement essay (if this is a part of the application). A student's personal statement should share their personal and academic experiences. Students should sell themselves and discuss their academic and extracurricular activities. Make those who are making the decision see what an asset a student would be to their university, and they will be proud to have the student as an alumnus when they graduate. These essays usually ask students questions about their abilities, goals, and talents. They may also ask the reason students wish to attend college in general and/or specifically attend their university. Some universities will want a recommendation from students' high school teachers or administrator. It is an excellent idea to have a teacher in mind to serve as a reference, and ask that teacher at least three weeks prior to the application deadline. Students should select someone who knows them well and who can attest to their academic ability. Most of all, select someone who is going to write a good recommendation letter.

There are several categories of admissions when applying to a university. If universities have a set number of freshman students to be admitted in each class, students may be placed on a wait list. Wait lists are a tool to keep a healthy pool of applicants. To be wait-listed does not mean that the student has been formally accepted to the university, but may be admitted if openings become available. This is usually a policy used at highly competitive universities. Some students may be accepted on a conditional basis. Conditional admission means that the university has accepted a student; however, the acceptance status depends on the student completing coursework or meeting specific criteria before enrollment or full acceptance. Conditional acceptance is a way for marginal students to prove that they are college ready. Open admission is a noncompetitive university admission where the only requirement is that applicants have a high school diploma or its equivalent to be admitted. This type of admission is usually used at community colleges or less competitive four-year colleges. Some universities use rolling admissions when admitting applicants to the university. Under rolling admission, candidates are invited to submit their applications to the university within a designated period of time, usually about six months. After this period ends, the university reviews applications and they let the applicants know if they have been admitted or not.

If parents want their children to think about and eventually attend college, it is never too early to ask them what college they plan on attending. Students should make the decision to attend college long before their senior year of high school. When a student enters into their freshman year of high school they should begin to seriously think about what colleges they should consider and they should think about what fields they might want to enter. While in high school students should take challenging courses in core academic subjects. That usually includes four years of English, three years of math and science, and three years of social studies. To become a more attractive college applicant, students should become involved in community service. Student athletes should ask questions of those who are attending college and college graduates. Students can gain valuable insight through these conversations and other mentoring-type relationships. They should participate in academic enrichment programs, summer workshops, and seminars to keep their skills sharp and gain new ones. Student athletes should look at the entrance requirements for schools in which they are interested. Students should narrow down the colleges to the schools that truly interest them and then make visits to these campuses. Then make a list of pros and cons about each school and decide which school fits their needs and budget. After a final decision has been made, then students should notify the school that was chosen and submit a deposit for a room in a residence hall. Students should also sign up for an orientation session and then attend the designated orientation session. Typically, when students leave the orientation session, they will have registered for their first semester of courses, and they are official college students.

Sports Science, Statistics, Analytics, Measurables, and Performance

Sports science is the systematic study of an athlete's health and safety. Through systematic study, an athlete's body is monitored to observe how it might react under certain stressors and conditions. In recent years, sports science and analytics have become a bustling, mainstream industry. The sports science industry is being used by some high-profile school athletic programs to make sure student athletes are performing at their optimal level while in competition. Coaches and recruiters look for many physiological characteristics when recruiting student athletes. They also look at indicators such as height, weight, length of arms, vertical jump, 40-yard dash times, and bench press to determine which athletes can perform at the top level of their sport. The research into the shape and size of elite athletes is showing some other, unexpected trends in other sports.

- Most elite swimmers have big feet and hands, long arms, short legs, and long torsos.
- Elite runners usually have abnormally long and skinny legs.
- Many elite tennis players have abnormally long forearms.
- It is common for elite baseball players to have almost superhuman eyesight and average hand-eye coordination.

It must be noted that if a student does not have the characteristic above or test well in certain athletic performance categories, it does not mean that he or she will not earn a scholarship. There is an old saying in athletics: "The big eye in the sky does not lie!" This means that videotaped performances of athletes show the true measure of how good an athlete is. There are several examples of athletes who did not have the measurable, were not the ideal size, and did not test well, but still earned athletic scholarships. Obtaining a college athletic scholarship is not about ability alone—it is about finding the right program, right university, and right coaching staff that bring the best out of their athletes.

Media Training

Media training teaches people the best way to interact with the media with the focus of obtaining good and positive media coverage. There are many benefits to student athletes to invest in media training. Many athletes should consider media training to help them gain the necessary skills when speaking with the media. Being polished and media savvy can improve the way they are perceived by perspective recruiters and the public in general. When a student athlete speaks on the radio or television, people are not only listening to the words that are being said, they are also looking at their facial expressions and overall body language. There is a wide array of judgments that can be made as a person observes an athlete's interview. During an interview, an athlete can come across as confident, arrogant, shy, or timid. They should try their best to have fun when giving an interview. These things may also play into a coach's evaluation of the student athlete. Being familiar with and trained to handle media attention will boost a student athlete's confidence. There are many people who are terribly fearful of speaking on television and radio or public speaking in general. Mastering the media can be a powerful form of showcasing a student athlete's skills and abilities.

There are several types of media interviews. Most common are the staged press interview, postcompetition interview, or featured story interview. The staged or press conference-type interview occurs after games or competitions and is held usually in a press room or a designated media area. Athletes should not chew gum or wear hats or headphones while giving an interview. A good interview can position some student athletes for a look from universities that are powerhouses in particular sports. Student athletes should try to anticipate questions ahead of time and use excitement when responding to questions. For the most part, questions especially after a sport's competition will be somewhat the same. They will have a lead in and then the question.

The following are after-game/competition questions that most athletes are asked at some time or another:

1. How do you think that your team performed tonight?
2. How do you feel about this victory and what does this victory mean to you?
3. How did you overcome the adversity that you experienced during the game?

Athletes are featured in interviews that may be a part of a television show or story in local or regional newspapers or magazines. These features may also be a regularly scheduled news program consisting of several short segments and various subjects of current interest to be examined, usually in greater detail than on a regular newscast. Regardless of the form of the feature, student athletes must cast themselves in the best possible light in these features. Featured interview questions may be more detailed than after-game/competition questions because the reporter wants to connect the athlete with the public and present details that may be otherwise not seen by those unfamiliar with the student athlete. Questions during a feature may be proposed on a deeper level or may be a lighthearted. The tone and questioning of the feature story really depends on the angle that the reporter or writer wishes. Questions in a feature story may consist of the following:

1. What kind of season do you anticipate?
2. What have you learned about teamwork?
3. What has influenced your work ethic?
4. When you are away from sports and school, what kinds of activities are you involved in?
5. What was it like growing up in your family and in your hometown?

6. At what age did you know that you were good at athletics and how did you know?
7. What do you want to do after you are finished playing sports?
8. What are your career plans or what do you plan on majoring in, in college?

At the beginning of an interview, an athlete should say "Hello" and shake the reporter's hand (if it is a one-on-one interview) and make eye contact with the interviewer. Also try to use the reporter's name at least once when responding to questions. A student athlete's response should be short and succinct. The athlete should master speaking in 15- to 20-second sound bites. When speaking with the media, especially after a game or competition, the student athlete must have a delicate balance of answering the reporter's question, while celebrating their own performance and teammates' performances. When discussing student athlete performances, students must be careful to not come across as arrogant or self-centered. If students witness most athletes, they should also lavish praise on their teammates and coaches. When talking about their teammates and coaches, call them by their names. This makes it personal and allows the student athlete to share the spotlight without being perceived as a selfish player. Always attempt to be positive and do not bring up negative issues, because coaches can Google most interviews and can use the interview to help in the decision whether to recruit or pass on an athlete. Do not allow reporters to put student athletes on the spot and make them uncomfortable with "gotcha type" questions. Most experienced media avoid asking these types of questions because they understand that there is a delicate balance between getting a good sound bite and embarrassing a young athlete. Student athletes should always maintain their composure during an interview and guide the interview where they would like it to go with their responses. In 2011, after a loss in the NCAA tournament, a reporter asked an athlete who had set a scoring record and carried his team to describe his emotions in the wake of a tough loss. The athlete broke down and began to sob. His coach had to intervene and reprimand the reporter by saying, "That is what you wanted to see? Is that what you were trying to get out of him? Make him cry here in front of people?" Afterward the coach sarcastically retorted, "Good question."

Athletes should not attempt to bluff their way through interviews. Be gracious in victory and defeat, always be positive and show class. Do not use the interview as an opportunity to talk trash about opponents. During an interview use common sense and do not use profanity or questionable language such as racial slurs or epithets during an interview. Student athletes should attempt to have fun during an interview. High school and college players should not respond to reporters the way Bill Belichick, Marshawn Lynch, and Gregg Popovich do. These individuals are at the pinnacle of their careers, and it has become a part of their persona and widely accepted by the media. However, dealing with the media as the aforementioned people have done could be detrimental to how student athletes are perceived by the media and the public. At the conclusion of any interview always say "Thank you."

Both male and female athletes are sometimes asked silly questions. An example of a silly question is, "Did you guys lose this game, or did your opponent win this one?" The best way to handle these types of question is to remain poised and not answer this question. Student athletes should not feel obligated to answer every question that they are asked. There is absolutely nothing wrong with saying, "I do not know" or "I cannot answer that question." This is better than saying "No comment." By saying "No comment," a student athlete has answered and led others to believe whatever they want to believe. Female athletes may get asked silly or inappropriate interview questions that their male counterparts will most likely not have to address. Inappropriate questions posed to female athletes may include questions about their dating lives, bodies, weight, and emotional capabilities. Other inappropriate questions for female athletes may include, "Why are you not smiling?" "Why did you wear this gear or outfit?" and "How long have you been playing against girls?"

Instead of asking questions, many reporters will attempt to use prompts to get athletes to discuss events from sports competitions like: "Can you talk about. . . ." "Can you describe. . . ." "Can you explain. . . ." "How important was it to. . . ." "Any thoughts on. . . ." These prompts can serve to allow athletes to elaborate in a freestyle type of response within the parameters of the reporter's prompt. Remember media training will train an athlete to control an interview, and this could work very well in concert with a reporter's promptings.

Undertaking media training will show athletes how to control the interview and make themselves look good. This is a subtle but important skill that can be learned and used effectively.

1. *Learn to speak in a way that people notice you in a positive way.* Your voice can be an instrument that can be used to magnify your athletic abilities and accomplishments. Use your tone, voice inflection, and body language to convey your confidence. An articulate athlete with exceptional abilities will get noticed.

2. *Speak clearly and concisely.* Practice enunciation and diction in front of a mirror. Avoid space "fillers" by saying, "you know," "um," and "ah" during an interview. By speaking in short simple sentences, this will assist in avoid saying "I mean," "um" and "ah." Also speaking clearly and concisely gives the appearance that you are articulate, and others may perceive you as intelligent.

3. *Anticipate questions and develop answers.* Watch pregame and postgame interviews of other athletes. Listen to the various types of questions reporters are asking and then practice how you would respond to that question. Practicing will not only make you better at interviewing, but it will also make you more comfortable.

4. *Learn to guide the interview.* Be composed at all times. During an interview, do not get angry or raise your voice in case it is captured on video. If an outburst is captured on video, you can be cast as a person without control of their emotions.

5. *Avoid saying things that can become bulletin board material.* During an interview, think before you speak. You should not speak badly about an opponent

or other competitors. Inflammatory remarks can give your opponent just enough motivation to defeat your team.

Social Media Training

While student athletes should obtain media training to maintain positive coverage in the media, they should also be trained in handling social media. Social media is a computer-mediated tool that allows people to create and share information about events, themselves, and others. It also allows individuals or groups to post photos and videos to virtual communities and networks. Social media relies on technology to create user-generated content. Social media can be a powerful tool as many have access to the information that is provided by users. Some coaches hoped that social media was a passing fad; however, it is here to stay in some form or another. Images and words cast on social media can be a powerful too, and it is closely tied with a university's athletic program's branding. All athletes, especially those who are in the age range of 18–24, are extremely active on all forms of social media. Since most high school and college athletes are living their lives under the scrutiny of the public, schools should train their athletes on what is acceptable and unacceptable to post on social media.

Some coaches have chosen to befriend their athletes on social media and monitor their activities and postings. Other coaches have chosen to prevent their athletes from using social media altogether. Student athletes and universities should become versed in the myriad of issues associated with social media and provide student athletes with the tools to make good social media choices. Among the issues that should be covered in social media training are privacy of information, pitfalls and traps, and cyber harassment risks. Most imperative, student athletes should be educated about the dangers of using social media irresponsibly and the impact and consequences that irresponsible use can have on their reputation and future careers. It is important to remember that once something is posted, the student athlete does not own it anymore—even if a student athlete deletes it, the social media company owns it.

Student athletes should Google themselves every now and again to see their digital footprint. They should remove every potentially inappropriate post and or picture. In any posting use correct grammar and avoid texting lingo in a public post. Student athletes must remember who they represent. It is not just about them; they represent many others. They are a representation of their family. Before posting any questionable material, student athletes should think how this post would affect their family and their reputation. Because many parents are proud of their child's academic and athletic accomplishments, they are affected by irresponsible actions on social media. Student athletes should make sure that their postings are true. Deion Sanders, Jr. tweeted, "Gotta get the hood doughnuts almost every morning. If my doughnuts don't come in a plain white box, I don't want them!" His tweet was retweeted 1,180 times and received 600 likes. When his father, NFL Hall of Famer Deion Sanders, saw his son's tweet, he set the record straight. The elder Sanders tweeted: "You're a Huxtable with a million $ trust fund stop the hood stuff! Lololol."

Student athletes represent people from their neighborhood and hometown and should remember this detail at all times. Their community is depending on them to make them look good. In certain communities, student athletes may be the topic of conservation at the barbershop, so make sure the conversation about them is positive. Give their community something to brag about. Student athletes represent their teams, and poor social media judgment can hurt their team and their school's reputation and athletic departments. Before student athletes post on social media, they should ask themselves, "Who will see this information on my social media pages?" Their team's opponent may see what they have stated on social media. This may provide them with the extra motivation needed to defeat the student athlete's team. Coaches will also see the things that are posted on social media. Disparaging comments may embarrass the athletic program and coaches affiliated with it. Unseemly social media comments can also be an embarrassment to families. Athletes' parents can often be the targets of undue media attention, criticisms, and taunts on social media. Athletes should make sure that they are not the cause of this negative attention by a mishap on their social media. The media also troll social media to look for an angle for future stories. It is best to not let social media posts be the headline or storyline in an article or television package that may cause people to question student athlete decision making and character. Athletes must also remember that future employers may see social media posts. Just because a social media post is deleted does not mean that it goes away. There are methods to retrieve deleted posts, and if others have received and saved the posts it will be fair game to use the post in evaluating the athletes' character and decision making. Not all student athletes will receive scholarships, and they must not let an ill-advised social media post become a part of the decision whether a scholarship offer is extended or not. Use social media in a positive way and give people a reason to follow student athletes on social media. Student athletes may do this by using social media to provide positive information.

On social media student athletes can keep those who follow them informed by providing updates of their progress such as 40-yard dash times, improved vertical jump, speed of their pitches, statistical information, or short video clips from game performances. Providing information can be used to keep potential recruiters informed of student progress. Student athletes can also use social media to motivate people. Even as a high school athlete, student athletes can motivate people to strive to be the best that they can be. Posting motivational slogans and sayings, especially those that have personally motivated them, can positively motivate others. For example, a quote by Vince Lombardi—"The difference between a successful person and others is not the lack of strength, not the lack of knowledge, but rather the lack of will"—or a quote by Derek Jeter—"There may be people that have more talent than you, but there's no excuse for someone to work harder than you do"—can serve to motivate someone to work a little harder. These are the kinds of quotes posted to a social media site that will serve as motivation.

A student athlete's post can also serve as inspiration for others. Motivational and inspirational quotes are similar. The difference between motivational and inspirational quotes is that an inspirational quote may have a general reference, may not be sports related, or may have a religious tone but can be used for motivation and inspiration. For example, you might post an inspirational quote by Pat Summitt: "Admit to and make yourself accountable for mistakes. How can you improve if you are never wrong?" An inspirational post may consist of a Bible verse such as Romans 8:28, "All things work together for the good of those who love the Lord and are called to His purposes." Another inspirational passage may come from the Quran such as Surah An-Najm, 53:39, "Man can have nothing but what he strives for." Social media posts may be used to congratulate others. By congratulating others on social media, this can show that the student athlete is an unselfish person and concerned about others and larger societal issues. It can show that they have an awareness and appreciation for the achievement of others. Student athletes should send kudos to other sports teams at their universities, especially those teams that may not receive as much attention as some of the high-profile sports teams. They should not post naked pictures of themselves or others or use profanity on social media accounts. Remember, future employers may look at a student athlete's tweets. Use the following as a rule: tweet things that you would say publicly and text things that you should say privately. This simple rule may save student athletes from enormous embarrassment.

Below are a few more wise actions when using social media:

Do Not Engage in Social Media Arguments

Student athletes usually come out on the worse end of these trivial electronic arguments.

Do Not Talk about Issues on the Team

Talking about team issues, especially those of a negative nature, can cause division within a team. There is a great chance that discussing team issues will destroy a team's chemistry.

Do Not Talk about Injuries

Discussing team injuries on social media may give your opponents insight to your team's game plan and aid them in their preparation.

Do Not Post Personal Contact Information

By not posting personal information, it will assist you in avoiding contact with overzealous fans or coaches. Having your personal information open also may leave you more susceptible to identity theft.

Do Not Post Your Whereabouts

If you are a high-profile athlete, there may be others who would like to cause trouble and may intentionally go to a place looking to cause trouble or start a fight with you.

Do Not Become Guilty by Association

As a student athlete, you should watch the people that you associate with and the organizations that you affiliate with. You should avoid those people or organizations that may put you in an adverse circumstance or situation.

No matter how great a student athlete is, no university's athletic program will be willing to invest a scholarship on an individual who will sully the brand of the university and its athletic program. This is why it is imperative that student athletes be aware how dealing with the media and negative social media can end their chance at getting a scholarship offer and derail a promising professional athletic career.

STEP THREE: PAYING ATTENTION TO THE ATTENTION

ESPN 100 and Other Rankings

There has been a proliferation of rankings of high school student athletes since the 1980s. During the 1980s, most of this information was compiled in national and regional sports magazines. Since the 1990s, there are many services that claim to help high school athletes get noticed by college coaches. Sites like Rivals, 247Sports, Scout, and ESPN may assist student athletes in getting noticed. Each of these entities has an individual or several people assigned to assist in constructing and updating recruiting information on their Web sites. These services may assist in helping set up profiles, but they are not always available to update Web sites with fresh statistics and other information.

Rankings

There are several systems that provide ranking information for high school athletes in particular sports, especially football. The most prominent lists come from ESPN, Rivals, Scout, and 247Sports. Each ranking system uses similar criteria to evaluate a recruit, but they all differ in the amount of weight each metric is given. All four services place a large emphasis on game film as a primary means of evaluating a recruit. Each system also grants a minimal value on scholarship offers, because few offers are actually "committable." Camps are typically understood as a space for confirming size and athleticism, rather than assessing talent. However, Rivals places great emphasis on using camps and 7-on-7 football drills as a means to evaluate talent, except for running backs and linebackers.

Camps

Despite the negative views of recruiting analysts, camps can be a beneficial way for high school athletes to generate attention that could lead to a potential scholarship offer. When it comes to attending camps, a student athlete must be proactive and attend the camps of the schools that have expressed interest. It is important for recruits to choose the right camp, such as those that provide a high level of exposure to college coaches who may offer a scholarship, as well as coaches who can elevate attendees to the next talent level. Invitations may come from a school or coach that has maintained contact and communication with a recruit, or from a school that has provided little, if any, communication. Receiving an invitation to a camp is not necessarily a sign of serious interest, because some camps may be public while others are invite-only. A public camp will likely post information on the college's Web site or it will send a brochure containing general information about the camp. An invite-only camp is more likely to send a letter directly from the school's athletic department to the recruit, signifying a targeted interest in that specific student athlete.

Staying Out of Trouble

Avoiding the pitfalls that can derail students from receiving a scholarship is a serious matter. There's no shortage of examples of student athletes making mistakes online. Of course it isn't just student athletes who make these mistakes, but they tend to be in the headlines more often. Profanity, arguing with fans, inappropriate pictures, suggestive comments, drug usage, underage drinking, offensive musical lyrics, and Snap Chat in an inappropriate or compromising setting—all of these are never-ending examples of poor choices aspiring collegiate student athletes can make. It is important to be aware that student athletes' online audience consists of more than just their friends. Be conscious that everything they post becomes public, whether or not it is something only meant for friends. One of the biggest mistakes student athletes make on social media is not realizing the potential magnitude of their audience.

Most people, specifically student athletes, fall into the trap of thinking that only friends or followers can see their posts, which leads to poor decisions. Social media is an extremely public place, and it is important to understand that individuals, including the media, do not necessarily need to have an account on most social media platforms to see what they are posting. As college programs increasingly use Twitter, Instagram, and other social media accounts to evaluate a player's character, one wrong comment can cost a scholarship offer. For example, an offensive line coach at a Big 10 school took to Twitter to vent his frustration with a recruit gone bad online: "Dropped another prospect this AM due to his social media presence . . . Actually glad I got to see the 'real' person before we offered him," the coach tweeted.

SUGGESTED READINGS

Bailey, Stephen. "College Football Recruiting: How Are Star Rankings Determined by ESPN, Rivals, Scout and 247Sports?" http://www.syracuse.com/orangefootball/index.ssf/2014/06/college_football_recruiting_stars_rankings.html

Carter-Francique, Akilah, Algerian Hart, and Astin Stewart. "Black College Athletes' Perceptions of Academic Success and the Role of Social Support." *Journal of Intercollegiate Sport* 6, no. 2 (2013): 231–246.

College Sports Scholarships. http://www.collegesportsscholarships.com/national-letter-intent-signing-dates.htm

Edwards, Harry. "Educating Black Athletes." *The Atlantic Monthly* 252, no. 2 (1983): 31–38.

Harrison, Walter. "NCAA Academic Performance Program (APP): Future Directions." *Journal of Intercollegiate Sport* 5, no. 1 (2012): 66–83.

Kingsbury, Alex. "The Great Campus Divide: The Dangers of Separating the Athlete from the Student." *U.S. News & World Report* (May 15, 2006). http://www.usnews.com/usnews/news/articles/060515/15duke.htm

McDowell, Jacqueline, Algerian Hart, and Emmett Gill. "Lingering Issues in Race and Leadership." In *Sport Leadership in the 21st Century*, edited by John F. Borland, 263–286. Burlington, MA: Jones & Bartlett Publishing, 2014.

National Collegiate Scouting Association Athletic Recruiting. "Sports Camps: Public vs. Invite-only." http://ncsasports.org/blog/2012/05/08/sports-camps-public-vs-invite-only/

Smith, Earl. *Race, Sport and the American Dream*. Durham, NC: Carolina Academic Press, 2007.

Smith, Earl, and C. Keith Harrison. "Stacking in Major League Baseball." In *African Americans in Sport*, edited by Gary Alan Sailes, 199–216. New Brunswick, NJ: Transaction Publishers, 1998.

PART III

Recruiting and Selecting the Right College Sports Program

STEP FOUR: EXPLAINING THE RECRUITING PROCESS

Questionnaires and Letters of Interest

In gathering information on student athletes, college coaches often use questionnaires to learn more about the student athlete. Student athletes should complete questionnaires from athletic departments. A questionnaire should be completed in clear handwriting or the form should be scanned and typed. The student athlete should proofread their responses to make sure that the responses are coherent and grammatically correct. When returning the questionnaire, it is a nice touch to return the questionnaire with a personal letter thanking the school for their interest. If a student athlete does not return the questionnaire, it will probably be perceived that there is not any interest and a university may remove the student athlete from their recruitment list. While a questionnaire may be an indication that there is some level of interest in a student athlete, a questionnaire does not indicate strong interest. It is always best to complete the questionnaire even for those schools that there may not be a strong interest in attending. If there are not any scholarship offers from schools of choice, there may be some interest from one of the universities that has the student athlete's questionnaire.

Letters of interest can be correspondence of a coach or athletic department's interest in a student athlete. Letters of interest can also be letters that student athletes send coaches in order to generate interest at a particular university. Letters of interest are not scholarship offers, but usually mean that a particular school has a student on a list of high school student athletes that the athletic program would like to evaluate. Some recruiters may even monitor the student's game statistics and competition results, but this does not mean that the student is being officially recruited. Some universities may mail out thousands of interest letters to high school athletes, but this not a scholarship offer nor does it mean that the school has a serious interest in the student. Student athletes are not officially being recruited until a recruiter makes contact with them and has a conversation about attending their college and competing in a particular sport at their university. Receiving a letter from a coach is simply a step in the recruiting game. Some of these letters may even been standard letters that are sent to any athlete that an athletic department may have a little interest in. If student athletes get a letter of interest, it is good. However, it should be noted that it is just a letter of interest, which may be the lowest level of interest. Below is a sample letter of interest from the NCAA Eligibility Center on behalf of the Collegiate Commissioners Association.

Sample

Administered by the Governing College Eligibility Center on behalf of the Collegiate Participant Organization (CPO).

Do not sign prior to 8 a.m. (local time) on the identified dates or after the imposed final signing date listed for each sport.

SPORT TYPE (Place an "X" on the specified line.) IDENTIFIED SIGNING DATE IMPOSED FINAL SIGNING DATE

_____

SPORT TYPE (Place an "X" on the specified line.)
Basketball (Identified Early Cycle) November 11, 2015–November 18, 2015

_____

Basketball (Identified Regular Cycle) April 13, 2016–May 18, 2016

_____

Football (Junior College Transfer) December 16, 2015–January 15, 2016

_____

Football (Identified Regular Cycle) February 3, 2016–April 1, 2016

_____

Field Hockey, Soccer, Men's Water Polo February 3, 2016–August 1, 2016 Track and Field/Cross Country

_____

All Other Sports (Identified Early Cycle) November 11, 2015–November 18, 2015

_____

All Other Sports (Identified Regular Cycle) April 13, 2016–August 1, 2016

IMPORTANT—READ CAREFULLY

Do not sign before reading this document in its entirety. Retain a copy for your own files and return one copy to the institution, which will then submit a copy to the proper conference office. Copies delivered via fax and e-mail will be considered valid. The National Letter of Intent is a system that the institutions and prospective student-athletes have entered voluntarily. Receiving aid and participation in athletics are not contingent upon signing the National Letter of Intent, either by a prospective student-athlete or his or her parents.

1.
Initial Four-Year Institution Enrollment. This National Letter of Intent only applies to prospective student-athletes who seek to enroll in a four-year institution for the first time. Prospective transfers who meet the requirements of the 4–2-4 designation, and who will graduate from a two-year college, are also able to sign the National Letter of Intent. No prospective student-athlete seeking mid-year enrollment will be allowed to sign the National Letter of Intent. The only exceptions are student-athletes in football who are seeking to transfer and have graduated midyear from a two-year college.

2.
Financial Aid. I must receive an offer, in writing from the institution named in this document, of athletics financial aid for the duration of the 2015–16 academic year at the time I sign this National Letter of Intent. The offer must identify terms, conditions, and the amount of athletics aid awarded. A two-year college football student-athlete seeking a midyear transfer must receive an offer in writing of athletics financial aid for the remainder of the 2015–16 academic year. The student-athlete shall be released from the institution does not renew the athletics aid for the following academic year. My parent/legal guardian and I must sign the National Letter of Intent for it to be considered valid (see institutional policy for parent/legal guardian signature). I must also sign the athletics aid offer sheet prior to submitting this National Letter of Intent to the institution named in this document. Any other stated conditions must also be met. This National Letter of Intent shall be declared null and void if the conditions stated on the financial aid offer are not met.

Professional Sports Contract. I remain bound by the National Letter of Intent in all sports even if I sign a professional sports contract in the sport in which I signed the National Letter of Intent, regardless of CPO rules that may prohibit the institution named in this document from providing me with athletics financial aid.

3.
Provisions of Satisfaction within the Letter.

a.

One-Year Attendance Requirement. The terms of this "above identified letter" shall be satisfied if I attend the college/university named in this document for one academic year (two semesters or three quarters) as a full-time student-athlete.

b.

Two-Year College Graduation. After signing the National Letter of Intent while in high school or during the first year of full-time enrollment at a two-year college, the terms of the National Letter of Intent will be satisfied upon the student-athlete's graduation from a two-year college.

4.

Basic Penalty. Understanding that if I do not attend the college/university identified in this document for one full academic year and I enroll in a different college/university participating in the National Letter of Intent program, I may not compete in intercollegiate athletics until I have completed one full academic year in residence at said institution. Additionally, I understand that I shall be charged with the loss of one season of intercollegiate athletics competition in all sports. This is in addition to all seasons of competition performed at any other institution.

5.

Early Signing Period Penalties. Prospective student-athletes who will participate in football are prohibited from signing the National Letter of Intent during the early signing period. A student who signs their National Letter of Intent during the early period in a sport other than football will be ineligible to practice or compete in football during the first year of enrollment at a National Letter of Intent member institution and shall forfeit one season of competition in football.

In circumstances where a student's primary sport is not football, but the student anticipates participating in football, the student should delay signing a National Letter of intent until either the football signing period or during the regular signing period for all other sports.

6.

Release Request and Appeal Process. In the event I wish to be released from my National Letter of Intent obligation, the National Letter of Intent release request form and appeal process information can be reviewed on the National Letter of Intent Web site at www.national-letter.org. I understand that the NLI Policy and Review Committee has been authorized to issue interpretations, settle disputes, and consider petitions for complete release from the provisions of the National Letter of Intent when extenuating circumstances are determined to exist and the signing institution denies my request for release. I further understand the Committee's decision may be appealed to the National Letter of Intent Appeals Committee, whose decision shall be final and binding.

7.
Letter Becomes Null and Void. This National Letter of Intent will become null and void should any of the following occur:

a.
Admissions Requirement. This National Letter of Intent will become null and void if I am notified in writing from the institution named in this document that I have been denied admission or, by the opening day of classes in fall 2015, has failed to provide me with written notice of admission, assuming I have submitted a complete admission application. It is my responsibility to provide, when requested, my academic records and an application for admission to the signing institution. Failure to submit the necessary academic credentials and/or application to determine an admission decision prior to September 1 will result in the National Letter of Intent being declared null and void. If it is discovered that I have intentionally failed to provide any and all required academic credentials to the institution, the National Letter of Intent office may determine the National Letter of Intent remain binding upon review. This National Letter of Intent will become null and void if I am eligible for admission, but admission is deferred to a subsequent term by the institution named in this document. However, If I defer admission, this National Letter of Intent remains binding.

b.
Eligibility Requirements. This National Letter of Intent will become null and void if I have not met the following before the opening day of classes in fall 2015: (1) the CPO initial eligibility requirements; (2) the CPO, conference or institution requirements for financial aid to student-athletes; or (3) the two-year college transfer requirements, contingent upon my submission of all necessary documents for eligibility determination.

(1)
This National Letter of Intent will become null and void if I am declared a non-qualifier (per Bylaw 14.3). This National Letter of Intent remains valid if I am a partial qualifier per CPO Division II Bylaw 14.3.2.1 unless I do not meet the policies for receipt of athletics aid at the institution.

(2)
It is my responsibility to register with and provide information to the Governing College Eligibility Center. Should I fail to submit the required documentation for an initial-eligibility decision and have not attended classes at the signing institution, the National Letter of Intent will become null and void. If discovered I intentionally failed to provide all required information to the Governing College Eligibility Center, the National Letter of Intent office may determine the NLI remain binding upon review.

(3)

This National Letter of Intent will become null and void if I am a midyear football two-year college transfer who fails to graduate from a two-year college at midyear (only for Division I nonqualifier). The National Letter of Intent remains binding for the following fall term if I graduated, met the two-year college transfer requirements for competition for the winter or spring term, and was eligible for admission and financial aid, but chose to delay my admission.

c.

One-Year Absence. This National Letter of Intent will become null and void if I do not attend any institution (two- or four-year) for at least one academic year, provided my request for athletics financial aid for a subsequent fall term is denied by the signing institution. I will be eligible to apply this provision if I originally enrolled in an National Letter of Intent member institution but have been absent for at least one academic year. To apply this provision, I must file a statement from the director of athletics at the institution named in this document with the appropriate conference office that such athletics financial aid will be unavailable for the requested fall term.

d.

Service in the U.S. Armed Forces/Church Mission. This National Letter of Intent will become null and void after serving active duty with the armed forces of the United States or an official church mission for at least 12 months.

e.

Discontinued Sport. This National Letter of Intent will become null and void if my sport is discontinued at the institution named in this document.

f.

Recruiting Rules Violation. If eligibility reinstatement by the CPO student-athlete reinstatement staff is necessary due to CPO and/or conference recruiting rules violations, I must be notified by the institution that I have an option to have the National Letter of Intent ruled null and void due to the violation. It is my decision to have the National Letter of Intent remain valid or declared null and void, allowing me to be recruited and not be subject to National Letter of Intent penalties.

8.

Recruiting Ban After Signing. I understand all participating conferences and institutions are expected to respect my signing and will not recruit me after signing this National Letter of Intent. I will alert any recruiter who contacts me that I have signed a National Letter of Intent. Once I have enrolled in the institution named in this document, the National Letter of Intent Recruiting Ban is no longer in effect and I shall be governed by applicable CPO bylaws.

9.

14-Day Signing Deadline. If my parent/legal guardian (see institutional policy for parent/legal guardian signature) and I fail to sign this National Letter of Intent and accompanying offer of athletics financial aid within 14 days after the designated date of issuance, it will be ruled invalid. In such a case, another National Letter of Intent may be issued within the appropriate signing period. Signing Deadline (November Only): National Letter of Intent must be signed between the dates of November 10–17, 2015 (the 14-day signing deadline is not applicable during the November signing period). Additionally, the National Letter of Intent must be filed by the institution with its conference office within 21 days of the date of final signature; otherwise, the National Letter of Intent is ruled invalid.

10.

Statute of Limitations. This National Letter of Intent will be in full force and effect for a period of four years, commencing with the date I sign this Letter. I am subject to the penalties of the National Letter of Intent if I do not uphold the agreement; however, once four years has passed, the National Letter of Intent is no longer binding.

11.

Coaching Changes. It is my understanding that I have signed this National Letter of Intent with the institution and not for a particular sport or coach. I remain bound by the provisions of this National Letter of Intent if a coach leaves the institution or the sports program (e.g., not retained, resigns). I understand it is not uncommon for coaches to leave their coaching positions.

12.

Coaching Contact Prohibited at Time of Signing. A coach or representative of the institution may not deliver this National Letter of Intent in person off campus, or be present off campus at the time I sign the National Letter of Intent per CPO rules. This National Letter of Intent may be delivered by express mail, courier service, regular mail, e-mail or by fax. An electronic National Letter of Intent submitted to an institution shall be considered a valid copy.

2015–2016

Name of Prospective Student-Athlete

_____

(Last)   (First)   (Middle Initial)

Permanent Address

_____

(City)   (State)   (Postal Code)   (Country)

___/___/_____

(Date of Birth)

(must have first registered with the Governing College Eligibility Center and on the List for Institutional Requests)

Prospective Student-Athlete's CPO ID _____

Date of Birth ____/____/_____

(must have first registered with the Governing College Eligibility Center and on the List for Institutional Requests)

Completion of this NLI has been authorized by:

SIGNATURE _____

Director of Athletics (or designee)

_____

Date Issued to Prospective Student-Athlete

Institution Use Only:
(Sport)

Two-year college transfer

____/____/_____

(Expected graduation date)

_____

(Name of Institution)

2–4 Qualifier or 2–4 Nonqualifier

____/____/_____

(Two-year college graduate expected graduation date)

This is to acknowledge my decision to enroll at

_____

(Institution Name)

I acknowledge that I have read all terms and conditions included in this document. I have discussed them with the appropriate representatives (coach and/or other staff) of the institution named above. I fully comprehend, accept, and agree to be bound by them. I understand that I am not required to sign the NLI to receive athletics aid and participate in intercollegiate athletics, and that signing this NLI is voluntary. Additionally, I consent to the signing institution, granting them the freedom to disclose to authorized athletics conference representatives (if any), in addition to the CPO, the CPO Governing College Eligibility Center and the NLI Office any documents or information related to my signing. Furthermore, I grant the NLI Office permission to disclose my name and personal information from my education records to a third party (including but not limited to the media). This shall be used as a means to correct inaccuracies reported by the media or related to my NLI signing. Such disclosure will not constitute a violation of my rights, including my rights under the Family Educational Rights and Privacy Act.

I understand I shall forfeit the first year of my athletics competition at any NLI participating institution if I falsify, or if I have knowledge that my parent or legal guardian falsified any part of this NLI.

My signature on this National Letter of Intent nullifies previous agreements, verbal or otherwise, which would release me from the conditions stated within this National Letter of Intent.

SIGNED _____

(additional text)

_____

(additional text)

Prospective Student-Athlete Signature Signing Date (Month/Date/Year) Time (a.m./p.m.) Appropriate U.S. Time Zones
Do not sign prior to 7:00 a.m.(check your time zone)(local time) on the initial signing date.
Parent/ legal guardian signature is required if prospective student-athlete has not reached his or her 21st birthday.

SIGNED _____

(text)

_____

(text)

Parent or Legal Guardian Signature Signing Date (Mth/Day/Yr)

(checkbox) Unchecked

(checkbox) Unchecked

Time (a.m./p.m.)

(check one) Do not sign prior to 7:00 a.m. (local time) on the initial (text) signing date.

_____

(text)

Print Name of Parent/Legal Guardian Telephone Number (including area code)

Student athletes may also write or e-mail a college coach expressing their interest in the athletic program or team. This correspondence is a way of introducing the student athlete to a prospective college coach. There are some athletes who have been overlooked or have not been discovered and a letter or an e-mail may get a student athlete noticed. The correspondence should be personalized, so the college coach knows that the student has a genuine interest in coming to their university. The letter or e-mail should also include contact information for the student and his or her high school coach. Coaches cannot contact students except during a designated period, and when contact is allowed, it may be very difficult if a student or the student's high school coach has not been included. It should also include the student athlete's athletic and academic abilities and accomplishments. The student athlete may also want to provide a schedule so that if the college coach chooses, they (or their representative) can attend to watch and evaluate the student athlete in person. Below is a sample letter of interest issued by a university.

August 1, 2013

Dear Prospect:

Congratulations, I would like to offer you the chance to receive an education and play college football at the highest level. Degrees from University ABC are among the most prominent in America. As the head football coach at this University, I want to formerly extend a scholarship offer to you.

My staff and I are committed to helping you develop your athletic skills. My coaching experiences have allowed me to coach and teach players from all levels, high school, college, and the NFL. You will learn the system and techniques that have benefited several players who have gone on to the next level.

Life-after-football opportunities are here for you at University ABC. The ABC experience affords you an outstanding opportunity to earn the letters NFL, CEO, or PhD. The education you earn lays the foundation for your professional life's work—a necessity in today's competitive work environment.

NCAA rules require me to tell you that for this scholarship offer to remain available to you, you must:

A. Successfully complete the requirements of your senior academic curriculum.
B. Meet all NCAA initial eligibility requirements that apply for your senior academic year.
C. Meet the admission requirements of University ABC.
D. Continue to live by the social rules that made you an outstanding student, athlete, and role model in your school and community.
E. Receive the recommendation of your high school coach.

University ABC football has a winning tradition. We want you to help us continue to win conference championships and an opportunity to play for a National Championship!

I want you on my team! Good luck to the entire Prospect football family this season!

Sincerely,

Coach

There also may be different levels of interest in a student athlete. Just because a coach expresses some interest does not mean that a coach has significant interest or an athletic department is going to make a scholarship offer. When an athletic department offers a scholarship in writing, it is the highest level of interest in a student athlete. However, there still must be a signed letter of intent that is returned to the offering school before it is official. Verbal scholarship offers, while they are a big step, are not a scholarship offer. Some coaches may make a verbal offer and most of them will not go back on their word, but to make it official there must be a signed letter of intent. If a school offers an official visit, this also indicates a level of interest. The official visit is a level below a verbal offer and a written scholarship offer. When an athletic department is willing to pay for a student athlete's trip to visit the school, this is an indication of interest. Some coaches may call student athletes on the phone. This also indicates an interest, but this interest may be only moderate. There may be a strong interest if a coach calls during the open recruitment periods. Phone calls also give student athletes an opportunity to learn more about the coach's personality and their staffs. Phone calls also give coaches a chance to learn about the student athlete and gauge their interest in their sports program.

Official Visits

After a student athlete's senior year, they may take an official visit to a university. An official visit is any trip that a student athlete and their parents take to visit a campus and some or all of the expenses are paid for by that university. This is usually an indication that this athletic program has a high level of interest in a student's talents as a student athlete. On an official visit this is an opportunity to evaluate the campus and inquire about athletic and academic opportunities at this institution. A student athlete and his or her parents should prepare a list of questions, so that he or she can truly see if that university is the best fit. According to the NCAA, student athletes can only make one official visit per school and only five total visits to all Division I schools. At Division II schools, there are an unlimited number of official visits.

Typically, on an official visit the host school will house the high school recruit with a student athlete on the team. Multiple athletes may show the recruit around campus. Most official visits last from 24 to 48 hours and usually include eating on campus, going to class, and engaging in some social activities, usually a party or gathering. The goal with an official visit is to show the student athlete the campus and show them various aspects of college life at this particular university. It is also good to remember that the host is observing the student and will probably be asked about his or her behavior while on the visit. Ultimately, this visit is to get the visiting athlete to choose this university, sign a scholarship if offered, and become a part of the school's athletic team.

Student athletes should consider how they dress while on their official recruitment visit. While shorts and gym shoes may be quite comfortable and these items seem to be the dress of choice for athletes, judgments are still made by how individuals dress. A student athlete should dress nicely and appropriately on their recruiting visit. This should continue as they enroll and become university students. Of course, it is an unreasonable expectation for college athletes to forego their athletic department–issued athletic gear, but it is a good general rule that it is better to be overdressed than to be underdressed. In any case, clothes should be clean, pressed, and fit properly, in order to give a good impression.

Student athletes must treat their official visit like a job interview. Those seeking jobs often research their prospective employers. Student athletes should research the recruiting university and its athletic department. They should also research the head coach and their position coach. Potential majors and minors at a university should also be researched because if the student athlete is serious about obtaining a degree, they should not sign with a school that does not offer a major or degree that they will seek. Prior to going on the visit, student athletes should think about questions that coaches and university players may ask while on their visit. Student athletes should then prepare short but detailed answers to their questions. It helps to put responses in the form of a story; this also helps students to remember the responses. It also gives the appearance that the student athletes are engaging. Make sure all responses are true.

On an official visit, student athletes should arrive at all events on time. If students are going to be late for the official visit, it is always a good practice to notify the coaches and athletic department. In most cases, athletic departments have an agenda for the visit and scheduled events, and meetings with various prospective university or athletic personnel. Therefore, it is imperative that the student notify the athletic department if he or she will be late for the visit.

On job interviews, employers watch the behaviors of those being interviewed. On an official visit, people will be watching the student athlete's behavior. Student athletes should be polite to everyone they encounter on their official visit. How an individual treats people says a lot about their character. Most coaches look for student athletes who are competitors and have character because that makes their jobs easier. On an official visit, student athletes should not engage in questionable activities that may endanger their eligibility, nor should they engage in illegal activities such as underage drinking or drug use.

Positive body language and an engaging personality are important on an official visit. Poor body language can cause coaches and those who are evaluating athletes to question if a student athlete is a good fit for their team. Detrimental forms of body language include slouching, looking off in the distance, playing with a pen, fidgeting in a chair, brushing back one's hair, touching one's face, chewing gum, and mumbling. These negative forms of body language should be avoided as much as possible. There are several forms of affirmative body language such as smiling, eye contact, solid posture, active listening, and nodding when interacting with individuals. Student athletes should practice affirmative body language before their official visit and also incorporate these behaviors in their everyday life.

After the official visit, the student athlete should write thank-you notes or send an e-mail to the coach and the athlete who hosted the student on the visit. It is a common courtesy and quite polite to thank those whom the student meets on the campus visit. Thanking people should begin while a student athlete is on their visit as they thank each person they meet during the visit. The student athlete's verbal thank you that is given on the official visit should be followed up with a written thank-you note or e-mail shortly after the visit. An official visit is a two-way interview. Student athletes are also interviewing coaches and other personnel and exploring the atmosphere of the university. On an official visit, student athletes and their parents should be prepared to ask numerous questions.

Lastly, some coaches make offers during a visit, but most coaches do not. If a coach does not discuss a possible scholarship offer, it is okay for student athletes to ask if they are being considered for a scholarship or if there are any academic or other scholarships available at the university. While on the visit, it is important for student athletes to ask themselves a very important question: "Is this university a place I would enroll even if I were not going to participate in athletics?"

Unofficial Visits

Making an unofficial visit to a college campus can be a fearful proposition as a young student athlete being recruited by a university's athletic program. Student athletes can become overwhelmed at a university because there may be so many more people and campuses can be so large, but official and unofficial visits can help the student athlete determine the best school for them. Visiting a campus can assist the student athlete in creating a list of what they want and do not want in an athletic program. More important, it will allow student athletes to determine if the university being visited is a good overall fit. Student athletes should take note of campus living and the campus atmosphere. Some high school student athletes may become familiar with a particular school because they have participated in competitions held at facilities on a particular campus. These student athletes may have also participated in camps sponsored by coaching staffs at a particular university.

The unofficial visit usually occurs prior to an official visit; however, this may not always be the case. On both visits, student athletes should be accompanied by their parents or guardian if possible. It is imperative for the student athlete to meet coaches at the prospective schools in which they wish to enroll. Student athletes should contact the coach and inform him or her that they would like to schedule an unofficial visit. Coaches will usually be very receptive. If a coach has viewed their play, they may give them an indication of their level of interest. If student athletes know a coach has watched them play, they should ask them where they stand on their recruiting list. Ask where they will be recruiting. For example, will they be recruiting at camps, conference events, all-star games, or tournaments? This information can potentially assist with coordinating a time for coaches who are unaware of their talents to see them play.

Sometimes a coach will ask student athletes to set up a visit themselves. In this case, make sure the coach has reviewed any available videos students may have prior to the visit. Ask the coach if they think the student should meet with the admissions office while visiting the campus. This will be an ideal opportunity to make a good first impression on the coach. Look clean and presentable—options may range from khaki pants or shorts to nice jeans, a casual dress or skirt, and a nice button-down shirt. Being prepared is essential when student athletes participate in a game-day visit. Game-day visits are typically unofficial and provide student athletes and their families with the opportunity to visit the campus and experience a live game as a spectator. Game-day visits are common most often in football recruiting; however, other sports participate as well. Remember, the coaching staff will be busy preparing their team and as a result recruits, at times, do not get as much one-on-one attention during game-day visits.

It is important to note that the accumulation of unofficial visits can be expensive. Prospects can, with few exceptions, visit a college campus at any time of the year. They can stay as long as they'd like and can see and do whatever they please. There's only one catch: The school can't pay for any of it. When an aspiring student athlete and his or her family visit multiple schools for unofficial visits they can expect to pay for flights, hotels, rental cars, food, and gas. A father of a four-star football recruit who took multiple unofficial visits racked up $14,000. Over this year of unofficial visits the family paid for:

flights: $6,092.40
hotels: $2,516.55
rental cars: $940.97
food: $3,151.25
gas: $1,810.70
for a **total**: $14,511.87.

While this example is on the higher end of the cost spectrum, it is important for aspiring student athletes and families to be conscious of unofficial visit costs.

Re-Cap Official vs. Unofficial Visit

The college pays for an official visit; the family pays for an unofficial visit. During an official visit, the NCAA allows schools to pay for lodging, transportation, meals, and entertainment. This can include airfare, rental car, three meals a day, tickets to three sporting events, and transportation to an off-site venue. The school cannot pay for parents. If a potential student athlete stays with a student athlete team member on campus, the coach cannot pay for their parents' hotel. On an unofficial visit, coaches can provide tickets to three sporting events with a value of $100.00. Official visits are prohibited until the opening day of class during the student athlete's senior year.

Host University and What to Look for on a Visit

A host university is the university that is hosting a student athlete and their parents for an official visit. The hosting university that is hosting an official visit for an athlete is allowed to pay for lodging, transportation, meals, and entertainment. Specifically, the hosting university is permitted to pay for three expenses: (1) round-trip transportation (rental car or airfare) for a potential student athlete between home or high school and the university's campus; (2) three meals per day for the student athlete and his/her parents; and (3) complimentary admissions to campus athletics events. It is important to note that just because a student athlete is being recruited and offered an official visit, this does not mean that a scholarship is being offered. This is an opportunity for the coach to make a judgment about the student athlete's lifestyle, personality, and character.

A host university's activities on a visit may vary depending on the school sponsoring the visit and the recruiting sport. Visiting student athletes are matched with a host and there is usually an itinerary set for the visiting student athlete and their parents. The itinerary is usually sent prior to the student athlete's arrival on campus. The host university may have a student athlete visit begin on Thursday evening (when the visiting student usually reports to the athletic department to meet the coach and their host) and last until Sunday. The host usually introduces the visiting athlete to other athletes for their sport and other student athletes from other sports. They usually show the athletic facilities including athletic complexes, sports venues, and residence halls. On Friday, the student athlete will have the opportunity to observe what a college class is like. The visiting athletes usually get the opportunity to shadow the hosting student athlete and sit in on their classes. They get to engage in many aspects of college life and should spend time in the student unions and cafeterias and tour the campus. Visiting student athletes will also meet academic support personnel and usually attend some social activities such as a sporting event or party. Student athletes should also make sure that they observe activities taking place on campus and in the city where the school is located. If there is not an item on the itinerary to visit the city, student athletes should ask.

Activities Student Athletes Should Engage in While on Their Visit

- Sleep in the residence halls and eat in the cafeteria
- Visit on- and off-campus housing
- Visit athletic training facilities and sports venues

- Visit various places off-campus in the city where the university is located
- Check out the library, labs, and study halls
- Meet coaches, trainers, and athletes from other sports
- Visit and observe classes and learn the academic culture of the institution
- Go out with future team members and ask questions

The host university is responsible for the student athlete's well-being. Student athletes should not be afraid to say "no" to any activities that are illegal or go against their personal moral code.

Student Athletes and Gifts

In recruiting, student athletes, their parents, or anyone claiming to represent the student athletes are prohibited from receiving any kind of gifts. Student athletes cannot receive payments as compensation based on athletic skill; this would be considered a preferential benefit that is not available to other students. The NCAA's policies prohibit student athletes from being represented by agents. After the student athlete's last collegiate game, then they may reach an oral or written agreement with an agent. The NCAA also disallows student athletes to request placement on a draft list.

The policy is somewhat different for basketball and football. In basketball, a student athlete may enter the draft one time during their college career without putting their eligibility in jeopardy. If the student athlete is not drafted, then they may declare their intention to start their college career again within 30 days after the draft. A Division I or Division IAA football student athlete can declare eligibility for the draft. If the student athlete is not drafted, the student athlete must declare his intention to return to college athletics within 72 hours following the National Football League draft, and the student athlete must write a letter to the university's athletic director.

Parental Involvement and the Role of High School Coaches

Parents should take an active role in the recruitment of their child. Some coaches may not want to deal with parental figures during the recruiting process and may choose not to pursue student athletes whose parents appear overbearing. While some may warn parents not to be a helicopter parent, it is the parent's duty to protect their son or daughter and to make sure they are making the best discussion for their future, particularly their careers after graduation and the cheering stops. Parents should become knowledgeable about college athletics and the recruitment process. Parents should learn what questions to ask, but more important, how to evaluate a coach's answers. In general, parents should ask questions, evaluate answers, fact check the answers, and then ask more questions.

Parents should not attempt to evaluate their son or daughter's talent. Parents can be quite biased in evaluating their child's talent level; they should leave this to those who are familiar with the attributes that it takes to compete at the college level. Of course, recruiters can be wrong in evaluating a student athlete's talent, and it is the parent's part to promote and get their student athlete's exposure to college athletic recruiters. Getting a son or daughter's name out to college recruiters may not be a high priority to some high school coaches. Most high school coaches are full-time teachers or administrators, so marketing athletes in the recruiting process may be a low priority. Parents should discuss with the high school coach their responsibility and what they are willing to do to assist in getting student athletes recruited by college coaches. Many high school coaches find the recruiting process very tedious. High school coaches can be an advocate or a hindrance in the recruiting process. Regardless of the sport in which a student athlete participates and whether student athletes like it or not, high school coaches play an important role in the recruiting process. High school student athletes should tell their high school coaches their goals early and make sure they are on board in helping to seek the best opportunity available. There will be highs and lows during the recruiting process and high school coaches should be available to help guide student athletes through this process.

College coaches will not only talk with high school coaches when gathering information about student athletes that they are recruiting, but may also talk with the principal and various teachers to ascertain what kind of person the student athlete is inside and outside of the classroom. When a high school coach receives letters for student athletes, these letters should be passed on to the student athlete. In some cases high school coaches have attempted to guide their student athletes to certain schools and may withhold letters or information from schools that they may not be fond of or dislike. Parents should stress to their son or daughter that they should not choose a school only because of the coach. Coaches come and go in college athletics. Even if a student athlete chooses a college because of a coach, this coach may take a job at another institution. Student athletes should pick schools because of the academics and how much they personally like the school.

Parents should make the official visits with their child. Parents should act as an extra set of eyes and ears. Watch the environment at the schools and watch their child's body language while they are on the visit. Parents should make sure that coaches are selling their entire campus and not just talking about their athletic programs. On an official visit if the coaches are selling and talking about athletics, this may be an indication that athletics may be more important than academics. Parents should keep notes on institutions visited and, when it is time to make a choice, should be involved in the decision making. Parents' wisdom can be invaluable in making a big decision like choosing the right college for their child. If parents do not feel as if they have enough information or experience to assist their child with making an informed decision, they should solicit the assistance of someone with experience to provide insight to make the best decision. Official visits can be expensive, so parents should plan wisely. Student athletes can receive up to five official visit requests, and these visits usually occur during a short period of time. It is cheaper to travel by automobile if possible. If the schools are too far to travel by car, parents should attempt to find inexpensive alternatives like bus or train. If there is not any other option and the student athlete has to visit the school alone, the student athlete should use FaceTime or Skype to communicate with their parents to ensure that they are a part of the visit even if they cannot be there physically.

Questions Student Athletes and Their Parents Should Ask Coaches

Below are some questions that a student athlete should ask while interacting with coaches and athletic personnel while being recruited.

- What is the team's practice schedule like and how many hours is it per week?
- What is the team's travel schedule like and how are academics handled when traveling with the team?
- How is the admissions process handled at the university? Are there preferences for student athletes?
- How many members of the team travel to away games or competitions?
- How are athletic activities and requirements balanced with academics at this university?
- What role do you see for me on the team? How will I fit in on this team?
- Why should I choose this school over the other schools that are recruiting me?
- What are the best features of your university?
- Where do you see this program in the next four or five years?
- How many people are currently being recruited?
- If I begin to struggle with academics, is there help to assist me with my classwork?
- Do athletic scholarships include work-study?
- Do athletic scholarships include books?
- How many credit hours can I take per academic year with this scholarship?
- What are some reasons I could lose my scholarship?
- Can you give me examples when student athletes have lost their scholarships?
- How are roommates chosen and how is housing determined?
- What is the cost of tuition, and room and board?
- Does the athletic department connect athletes with potential summer employment or internships?
- What are the scores on the SAT or ACT required for unconditional admission into your university?
- Is there a full-time strength and conditioning coach on the staff?

- Is there a full-time team medical doctor and full-time trainers to assist me if I get injured?
- What is the team's conditioning program during the season and off-season?
- Typically, when does the academic school year begin and end?
- Will a fifth year be provided under scholarship, especially if graduation is close?
- If a career-ending injury occurs, are there opportunities to remain on scholarships?

Parental involvement in recruiting and selecting a college is imperative. Parents who are involved in the recruiting and selection process make coaches understand that their child is not just a commodity but a person.

Benefits of Parental and Guardian Involvement in the Recruitment Process

- It allows parents to learn about the university and the atmosphere in which their son or daughter will be living and competing.
- It allows parents to learn how the coach treats and interacts with players.
- It allows parents to become knowledgeable of the coach, coaching staff, and their philosophy.
- It allows parents to make the coaches aware of their expectations regarding their son or daughter.
- It makes coaches aware that the parents' son or daughter cannot be viewed simply as a commodity.
- It allows coaches to learn a student athlete's family's values.
- It allows parents to help the student athlete to make the best choice and fit for them.

Recruiting should be a multiperson task and a family-oriented event. However, it is ultimately up to the student athlete to decide where they will attend college and continue their athletic career. While this huge decision might be a frightening idea for some student athletes and their parents, parents must be a part of the process and assist their child in making the best decision. There is absolutely nothing wrong with parents having input into this decision. Parents should be wary of any coach who does not want them involved in the recruiting process.

STEP FIVE: DELIBERATING ON AN ATHLETIC SCHOLARSHIP OFFER

Verbal Commitment

A verbal commitment is when a prospective student athlete recruit agrees to accept a scholarship and participate in a particular sport if offered from a particular university. Specifically, it is when a student athlete publicly states one's intentions to attend a certain institution, and is a nonbinding oral agreement between a high school student athlete and the institution. The only binding nature of the commitment is the word of the student athlete and the university's promise. It is not uncommon for a student to verbally commit to one university and then change their mind and sign a National Letter of Intent with another university. Sometimes, a university may accept a student athlete's verbal commitment and later offer a NLI to another student athlete.

Coaches may pressure high school student athletes into issuing a verbal commitment so that competing coaches will end their efforts to recruit a student athlete. Student athletes should think long and hard before issuing a verbal commitment. *Decommitment* is when a student athlete changes their mind and decides to redraw their commitment from one university and decides to commit to another university. Though commitments are nonbinding, the student athlete's character may be called into question if several verbal commitments are issued or if the student athlete decommits multiple times. Some student athletes make verbal commitments as early as their sophomore year of high school to avoid the hassle of recruiting wars. It is important to note that only a signed National Letter of Intent along with a financial aid agreement is a binding agreement.

National Letter of Intent

A National Letter of Intent (NLI) is a legally binding contract. Student athletes should not sign a letter of intent until they are fairly certain that they have an understanding of the purpose of this letter. The letter of intent should be signed and sent to the student athlete before the official signing period starts. Student athletes and their parents must make sure that they are aware of the specific deadlines of their particular sport's signing period, and the student athlete has only 14 days from the date that the national letter is received to sign it. The NLI must be sent through fax or through e-mail. On the NLI, the university's athletic department should complete the top half of the letter of intent and the recruit must sign the bottom half of the document. If the university does not complete the top half of the letter of intent properly, then the letter of intent is invalid or it may not be a letter of intent at all. If the student athlete is under age 21 years old, their parent or legal guardian must also sign the NLI. Student athletes cannot sign a letter of intent before 7:00 a.m. on the first day of the signing period for the appropriate sport. University coaches are prohibited from delivering the NLI or to be present at the signing of the letter of intent.

There are several parts of a NLI. For student athletes signing directly out of high school, the first portion of the NLI provides that it is the intent of the student athlete to enroll into the university for the first time. Midyear junior college transfers in football may follow a different process. The NLI will also include a financial aid requirement. This section ensures that the student athlete's NLI also has a scholarship agreement included. Only players receiving scholarships sign NLIs.

If a student athlete plans to walk-on at a university, they are not required to sign a letter of intent. A NLI contains information on what is expected of the student athlete. Specifically, by signing a NLI, the student athlete is agreeing to attend the university for one full academic year and participate in a particular sport. For junior college athletes there are additional requirements. Junior college athletes have to attend a four-year university for one full academic year or have graduated from a two-year college to sign a NLI.

Student athletes must remember that a NLI is a contract with a university and its athletic department. If a NLI is signed and the student athlete does not play for the school in which the NLI was signed, then the student athlete cannot play for another university for one full academic year. Also, the student athlete's eligibility is lost for a full year in all sports. If a release can be obtained from the school for which the letter of intent was signed, then a student athlete may be eligible to sign a scholarship with another university and participate in sports. In most cases, university athletic programs will grant a full nonconditional release to athletes to allow them to resume their athletic careers elsewhere. Some university athletic programs grant releases with conditions attached to them. One of the most common term of conditions is to dissolve the letter of intent but not allow the student athlete to transfer to a competitor within their athletic conference or a noted rival. Requesting to be released from a NLI is classified as a 4–4 transfer. In the cases of a 4–4 transfer, the student athlete seeks to break his or her NLI to sign with another university. There are cases where a NLI can be declared null and void. A NLI can be voided for the following reasons:

- The student athlete is not admitted to the university;
- The student athlete is a nonqualifier;
- The student athlete does not attend the school with which they signed the NLI agreement;
- The student athlete joins the military or goes on a church mission;
- The student athlete's sport is discontinued at the university; and
- A university's recruitment activities while pursuing student athlete violate NCAA rules and policy.

Once an NLI is signed, the recruitment process has concluded for the student athlete being recruited. Student athletes should understand that once a NLI has been signed with a university, coaches from other universities are prohibited from continued recruiting. It is important to note that the NLI is a contract with the university not the coach of the athletic team. If the coach leaves or is fired, the student athlete is still obligated to attend the university. They may seek a release; however, they should meet the new coaching staff before hastily seeking a transfer to a new school.

Multiple Sport Student Athletes

At one time, multiple sport collegiate athletes were common. In the modern era, rarely do student athletes get to compete in multiple sports during their college career because athletes have become more specialized and only focus on one sport. There are several examples of multiple sport athletes in college. At Syracuse University, Jim Brown competed in both football and lacrosse; at Auburn University, Vincent "Bo" Jackson competed in football, baseball, and track; at Florida State University, Deion Sanders competed in football and baseball; and Jameis Winston competed in football and baseball. These are examples of student athletes who chose to continue to participate in multiple sports and were successful in both sports.

The NCAA has policies and rules used to govern multiple sport athletes. According to the NCAA, for a student athlete to be considered a multiple sport athlete, they must meet all of the following criteria:

- The student athlete must report and actively participate in regularly organized/ scheduled practice with each squad;
- All student athletes shall participate where qualified in official competition in each sport;
- The student athlete shall be a member of each team for the duration of the defined playing and practice season; and
- If an individual is a recruited student athlete, said individual shall have been earnestly recruited to participate in the sport in which financial aid is counted.

The institution to which the student athlete has been recruited must have a reasonable belief that the student athlete can participate in multiple sports and they should provide documentation that the student athlete has previously participated in those specific noted sports. In addition, a student athlete must be certified as a multiple sport athlete with the NCAA. In the past, many universities skirted the multiple sport policy by recruiting student athletes to receive a scholarship or grant-in-aid and compete in one sport while being counted as a walk-on in another sport. This was a practice used to by-pass the NCAA sport financial aid limits with special multiple sport student athletes. Basketball, football, baseball, volleyball, and track and field were the most common sports used to skirt the NCAA multiple sport rule. Today the multiple sport student athlete is rare at the Division I level, but probable at the Division IAA and II level. It is important for prospective student athletes to inquire about multiple sport scholarship opportunities because they can offset the cost of attending college.

College Coaches' and Athletic Departments' Antics to Seal the Deal

Recruiting has become very competitive. Increasingly, college coaches and athletic departments have been doing whatever it takes to lure recruits into signing with their schools. It has become common for coaches to move out of their comfort zones and say "Yes" in order to seal the deal with recruits. Coaches and universities have become creative and have shown their personality in attempting to win recruiting battles. Coaches have been seen on social media doing the latest dances, playing games, and attending family parties to win over a recruit's family. Coaches from the University of Alabama and the University of South Carolina have been requested to dance at family gatherings of a recruit. The University of Georgia head coach brought a bulldog puppy (the school's mascot) to a recruit's home, while the University of Notre Dame's athletic department sent an 18-wheeler equipment truck emblazoned with the university's logo to a recruit's house.

Coaches and athletic departments are going through great lengths to get recruits to commit to their schools. For example, the Clemson University athletic department sent a recruit's mom a birthday cake in the school's colors and shaped like a jersey with the recruit's jersey number on it. Another coach began recruiting the recruit's girlfriend to come to the school on an academic scholarship. The University of Houston used celebrities and sports stars to welcome their recruits after they officially signed their letters of intent. Louisiana State University put billboards with the face of each recruit all over the state. The coach at the University of Michigan even went so far as to honor the request of a recruit's younger sister and climbed a tree in the recruit's front yard. Most recruits know that they cannot base their college decision on whether a coach will engage in their requests or somewhat embarrassing antics. Coaches have learned that in winning top recruits, they must let their guard down and show their personality because it appears that young student athletes prefer to play for those coaches who show their human side in recruiting.

Deliberating and Making a Decision

What should student athletes and their families consider when narrowing and making their final decision of college choice? There are not any guarantees in life. Student athletes and their families should identify the objectives in accepting a scholarship offer. Is the objective to turn professional after eligibility has expired? Is the objective to turn professional as an underclassman? Is the objective to use collegiate athletics as a means to obtaining an undergraduate degree in a chosen field? Student athletes should do their homework when deliberating multiple scholarship offers. Gather as much information about the university, coaches, athletic department, and location of the school. The student athlete must determine if the athletic department's values are congruent with their own value system. Make a list of pros and cons for each school and prioritize which considerations are more important and which are less important. Solicit input and feedback from trusted people. Parents can be invaluable because they often think of things that the student athletes have not considered.

Things to Consider

- Does this scholarship cover my entire cost of college, i.e., cost of attendance, fees, and housing?
- Does this university have the major and minor that I want?
- How does the coaching staff treat their athletes?
- Would I attend this school if I were not receiving a scholarship offer?
- What are my other scholarship opportunities other than athletic scholarships?
- If I am a multiple sport athlete, what are my opportunities to participate in one or more sports?
- Is this school under investigation by the NCAA and how does this impact the athletic program?
- What is the graduation rate of athletes at the school that I am considering?
- Does the scholarship cover courses during summer sessions and winter session?

STEP SIX: MAKING IT OFFICIAL: SIGNING DAY AND THE SIGNING DAY PRESS CONFERENCE

National signing day is when high school student athletes can sign an NLI to play college athletics at particular universities. Making national signing day an event has become a very big deal since the early 1990s. For football, national signing day is the first Wednesday in February. Several coaches proposed national signing day, a resolution was presented to the NCAA and adopted in 1980, and the first national signing day took place in 1981. Prior to the uniform signing day, various athletic conferences, in particular the Southeastern Conference and the Atlantic Coast Conference, held signing day on the second Saturday in December. Some people really dislike the spectacle that national signing day has become, while others love the ceremony of it.

It has become customary in college athletic recruiting for blue-chip athletes to announce their college selection in very elaborate ways. Most have a signing day press conference. The hat ceremony is a signing day press conference event that has become very popular in announcing the student athlete's intentions. Usually this event takes place in an auditorium or some other venue where fans and fellow students can witness the signing day press conference. This should be an event planned and publicized at least two weeks in advance. Flyers publicizing the signing event need to be passed out and the local media should be invited. This should be followed up with a personal phone call to provide any additional information concerning the event. The press conference area should be staged at least an hour before anyone is expected to arrive. The area should include a podium or table with the student athlete's high school's team logo on it. If a podium is not used, use a long table and chairs if more than one speaker will be participating. If possible the table should have a table cloth featuring the school's logo on it. Remember to set up seating for the expected number of attendees and test microphones, sound systems, and lights. It is imperative that the signing day press conference starts on time. Student athletes should either read a prepared script or make a short statement before announcing their college choice. At the signing day press conference, it is important that the student athlete thank all of those who have contributed to their success.

Usually there are attempts to shroud this event in secrecy about the selection to add intrigue and mystery to the event. One recruit even jumped out of an airplane to announce his college intentions. Another recruit used his friends and a paintball course to announce his intentions. Some recruits have made polished videos to make their announcements while others have been invited to ESPN studios to announce their college choice.

At the hat ceremony, several baseball caps are placed on a table and the student athlete reads a statement and puts on the cap of the school that he or she has selected. The student athlete then signs their letter of intent. The most important part of this signing day press conference is to make sure that the letter of intent is faxed or e-mailed to the college's athletic department.

Essential Items Needed to Stage a Signing Day Press Conference

- A place to stage the event, sound system, and table or podium
- Invitations sent to the media and various people
- A prepared script
- Access to a fax machine or scanner and e-mail
- A writing utensil
- The letter of intent from the university
- A camera for personal photographs

Some student athletes have chosen a low-key approach to announcing their intentions. They chose to not hold an elaborate signing day press conference. They have turned to social media to announce where they will attend school by using Facebook, Instagram, Snapchat, or Twitter. Student athletes and their parents should realize that a signing day ceremony is a public acknowledgment of an opportunity at obtaining a college education.

Opportunity

A college athletic scholarship is an opportunity. While student athletes often focus on the glory of college athletics, they must remember that it is also an opportunity to earn a college degree. Many boys and girls grow up dreaming of playing sports in the collegiate and professional ranks. According to the NCAA. org, "of the nearly 8 million students currently participating in high school athletics in the United States, only 480,000 of them will compete at NCAA schools.

And of that group, only a fraction [fewer than 2 percent] will realize their goal of becoming a professional athlete."

For the others, the experiences of competing in college athletics and the life lessons they learn along the way will help them as they pursue careers in other fields. Education is a vital portion of the college athletics experience, and student athletes must treat it that way. Overall, student athletes graduate at higher rates than their peers in the student body, and those rates rise each year.

Athletic scholarships for aspiring student athletes are competitive, because, like most merit-based financial aid, they are awarded to recognize high achievement. On the other hand, grants like those disbursed by the federal financial aid program are usually awarded based on need, rather than performance. Campus financial aid administrators use scholarships and grants to establish funding for star athletes, who increase their own access to student assistance by maintaining winning combinations of scholastic excellence and outstanding athletic achievement.

Scholarships for athletes originate from a wide variety of public and private benefactors, including athletic organizations, foundations, corporations, individual universities, women's groups, and minority advocacy associations. A student athlete's access to college assistance is influenced by where they go to school, their academic major, the sport in which they excel, and a host of personal characteristics connected to their academic and athletic success. Passion, commitment, talent, and drive open doors to marquee athletic scholarships, as well as college funding for students who compete at smaller colleges and universities. In addition to athletic performance, scholarship eligibility takes into account.

SUGGESTED READINGS

Brooks, F. Erik, and Glenn Starks. *African American College Student's Guide to Success*. Santa Barbara, CA: Greenwood, 2015.

Etzel, Edward. *Counseling College Student-Athlete Issues and Intervention*. Morgantown, WV: Fitness Information Technology, 2006.

Hayes, Andre, and Vince Fudzie. *Your Brain Is a Muscle Too: How College Athletes Succeed in College and in Life*. New York: Harper Collins, 2013.

Petrie, Trent A., and Eric L. Denson. *A Student Athlete's Guide to College Success: Peak Performance in Class*. Belmont, CA: Wadsworth, 2002.

Zagelman, Adam. *School Counseling and the Student Athlete: College, Careers, Identity, and Culture*. New York: Routledge, 2014.

PART IV

Receiving a Scholarship, Student Athletes, and the Rules

STEP SEVEN: EXAMINING THE INS AND OUTS OF A COLLEGE SCHOLARSHIP

Scholarships

Student athletes must be aware that receiving a scholarship offer does not automatically equate to a full scholarship. Instead, scholarships are typically annual contracts that are renewable yearly with no guarantee for multiple years. Full scholarships are more readily available in head count sports, and they enable recipients to attend college at little cost. Full scholarships typically cover tuition, room and board, books, and certain university fees.

Common Myths

There are several beliefs about athletic scholarships that are often misinterpreted or misunderstood. Some people believe that all scholarships are full offers, coaches will find athletes to recruit, academics are less important than athletic ability, athletes do not have the talent to earn a scholarship, and that scholarships last all four years. Despite the popularity of these beliefs, they are inaccurate. First, not all scholarships are full-ride offers, as most are only available in head count sports. Second, coaches do not typically seek out every athlete they recruit. Coaches do not have time to travel around looking for athletes. They need information from student athletes in various forms, including an athletic résumé, academic information, and a personal cover letter. Athletes can also join Web sites and services that provide easier access to coaches when looking for athletes to recruit. The third misconception is that academics are not as significant as athletic ability. However, academics are just as important as athletics, because student athletes must meet NCAA eligibility requirements each semester or quarter. Fourth, most student athletes believe they are not talented enough to earn a scholarship.

While very few athletes are able to compete at the Division I level, there are still multiple opportunities for athletes at all levels. Student athletes should consider all options, including Division II, Division III, NAIA, and junior college sports. The fifth common myth about scholarships is that they last all four years. This is far from the truth as most scholarships are year-by-year deals that are renewed by the coach and the school at the end of the year. A scholarship does not guarantee money for a student athlete's collegiate career, because it is subject to possible changes and withdrawals based on performance.

Choosing the Right Opportunity

Student athletes who wish to compete in college sports should create a list of about 75 percent dream schools and 25 percent safety schools. Dream schools are the schools a student athlete hopes to attend, but would need assistance to qualify for the financial, academic, or athletic standards. Some schools may be listed as a dream school if a student athlete is not athletically ready to play at a particular level, needs help with grades and test scores, or cannot afford tuition without a significant scholarship. Safety schools are the schools that are more likely to accept a student athlete and allow them to play. In order for a school to be considered safe, a student athlete should meet the academic qualifications, receive an honest third-party assessment of their athletic ability, and consider the ability to pay tuition and the full cost of living without receiving aid from an athletic scholarship.

STEP EIGHT: NAVIGATING THE NCAA POLICIES AND PROCEDURES

Remaining Eligible: Academics

NCAA.org provides many examples of important rules aspiring NCAA-governed student athletes must know. Intercollegiate sport is part of the fabric of the university: within this space, the student athletes must be committed to academic success while matriculating toward degree completion. Student athletes must balance between meeting academic standards and athletic performance. Throughout the career of a student athlete they must remain eligible to actively participate in intercollegiate athletics. All NCAA member institutions in each division create academic standards specific to that division's goals. According to the NCAA.org, in Division I, student athletes must complete 40 percent of the coursework required for a degree by the end of their second year. They must complete 60 percent by the end of their third year and 80 percent by the end of their fourth year. Student athletes are allowed five years to graduate while receiving athletically related financial aid. All Division I student athletes must earn at least six credit hours each term to be eligible for the following term and must meet minimum grade point average (GPA) requirements that are related to an institution's own GPA standards for graduation.

All sports programs and teams across Division I are subject to the Academic Progress Rate (APR), which is the "standard that measures a team's academic progress by assigning points to each individual student athlete for eligibility and retention/graduation." Within Division II, student athletes must complete 24 credit hours toward their degree each academic year to remain eligible for competition. At least 18 of their credit hours must be completed between the beginning of fall classes and into spring commencement at their institution (additionally: six hours may be earned in the summer). Those participating as Division II student athletes must earn a minimum of six credit hours every term to remain eligible for the following term.

The GPA requirement for Division II student athletes is they must earn a 1.8 cumulative GPA after earning 24 credit hours, a 1.9 cumulative GPA after earning 48 credit hours, and a 2.0 cumulative GPA after earning 72 credit hours to maintain eligibility. Student athletes have 10 semesters of full-time enrollment to use over the duration of four seasons of competition, so long as they maintain academic eligibility. All Division II student athletes must complete their four seasons of competition in their first 10 semesters of enrollment, or the equivalent of 15 quarters of full-time enrollment.

According to the NCAA.org:

> While there are no minimum national standards for establishing or maintaining eligibility in Division III, student athletes must be in good academic standing and make satisfactory progress toward a degree as determined by the institution.
>
> Division III student athletes must be enrolled in at least 12 semester or quarter hours, regardless of an institution's own definition of "full time." (http://www.ncaa.org/student-athletes/current/staying-track-graduate).
>
> Institutions in all divisions must determine and certify the academic eligibility of each student-athlete who represents the school on the field of play. Institutions are responsible for withholding academically ineligible student-athletes from competition.
>
> Waivers are available for many of these rules, including progress-toward-degree standards.
>
> Student-athletes who are declared academically ineligible must use the student-athlete reinstatement process to be restored to competition (http://www.ncaa.org/remaining-eligible-academics).

Division I Governance

Division I in recent times redesigned its system of governance to create a structure that is more efficient and applicable to be more responsive to membership needs. The NCAA Division I member institutions adopt governing bylaws through two legislative processes. The two systems are referred to as Autonomy and Council Governance. Each process includes significant influence and input from member presidents and chancellors, directors of athletics, athletic administrators, coaches, faculty athletic representatives, conference commissioners and personnel, and the student athlete participants from Division I schools and conferences. All NCAA committees populated by membership personnel conduct their division's daily operations and business to establish strategic direction for the future of competition among membership. The membership receives invaluable assistance concerning all areas of competition and compliance from the NCAA staff at the national office.

The NCAA's Division I committee structure includes everything from managing championships and sport oversight, to strategic planning and the general health and wellness of its body. As identified by the NCAA national office:

> The student-athlete voice is an important component of the Division I governance structure. Two members of the Division I Student-Athlete Advisory Committee participate and vote in meetings of the Division I Council, the division's primary policy-making body. The Student-Athlete Advisory Committee also has a voting student-athlete on each of the seven standing committees of the Council. Students also participate actively in the autonomy governance structure. Conferences choose 15 student-athletes to be part of the 80 votes cast on autonomy legislation.

Many potential regulations and proposals to change existing policies are developed within the committee governance structure throughout the year, while other legislative measures are proposed by member conferences. Proposals (via committee or through the membership) must annually be submitted to the national office by September 1. All Division I members are allowed to comment on proposed legislation for 60 days. However, there is an amendment time period between November 1 and November 15. The entire Division I membership receives official notice on all proposals and amendments by December 1. The membership has the right to comment on proposals and amendments from this time until voting. The autonomy structure votes on its proposed legislative slate at an identified business session. The council governance structure votes on its proposed legislative slate during its membership meeting/s in April. All bylaws and regulations are published annually in the NCAA Division I Manual, the division's official governing rulebook.

Staying on Track to Graduate

As discussed previously in the guide book, success in the classroom is just as important as winning on the field. The NCAA has created standards that help to ensure student athletes make progress toward degree completion every year and every season. Student athletes are required to meet these standards to remain eligible to participate in collegiate sports. All NCAA members have set separate standards that reflect the philosophies and goals of each division.

Division I

Forty percent of a student athlete's required coursework for degree matriculation must be completed by the end of their second year. Sixty percent of a student athlete's required coursework for degree matriculation must be completed by the end of their third year, and 80 percent by the end of their fourth year. Student athletes are allowed five years of eligibility and athletically related financial aid. All Division I student athletes must earn at least six credit hours every term to be eligible for the subsequent term in addition to fulfilling the minimum GPA requirements as defined by their institution's GPA standards for graduation.

Division II

Twenty-four credit hours toward a degree must be completed every academic year for student athletes to remain eligible. According to the NCAA, a minimum of 18 hours

must be earned between the beginning of fall classes and spring commencement, and up to six hours can be earned in the summer.

All Division II student-athletes must earn at least six credit hours each full-time term to be eligible for the following term.

Student-athletes must earn a 1.8 cumulative grade-point average after earning 24 credit hours, a 1.9 cumulative grade-point average after earning 48 hours and a 2.0 cumulative grade-point average after earning 72 hours to remain eligible.

Division II student-athletes must complete their four seasons of competition within the first 10 semesters or 15 quarters of full-time enrollment. (http://www.ncaa.org/student-athletes/current/staying-track-graduate).

Division III

It is important to note:

While there are no minimum national standards for establishing or maintaining eligibility in Division III, student-athletes must always be in good academic standing and make satisfactory progress toward a degree as defined by the institution.

Division III student-athletes must be enrolled in at least 12 semester or quarter hours, irrespective of their institution's own definition of "full-time."

Waivers are available for many of these rules, including progress-toward-degree standards (http://www.ncaa.org/student-athletes/current/staying-track-graduate).

Why Do Academic Standards Vary Among Divisions?

All NCAA member institutions select to associate with the division that most closely reflects their specific institutional values and mission. Just as each institution has a unique set of characteristics that attract a diversity of students, each NCAA division is distinctive and has its own requirements.

Why Are Division I and II Student Athletes Required to Complete a Certain Percentage of Their Degree Each Year?

One of the core goals of the NCAA is to integrate athletics with academics. With this essential focus, the memberships in Divisions I and II have approved eligibility standards intended to maximize graduation rates while minimizing incongruent effects on economically disadvantaged groups. The Division I standards currently in place (both percentage of degree requirements and minimum GPA standards) are supported by data that show student athletes who are most likely to graduate will in fact meet these standards.

STEP NINE: ADJUSTING TO COLLEGE LIFE AND COLLEGIATE ATHLETIC COMPETITION

Classifying Terms of Eligibility Status

The NCAA has many classifying terms to define incoming student athletes' eligibility status. There are "redshirts," "greenshirts," "grayshirts," and "blueshirts." These classifying terms are usually used in football. Players who redshirt are able to participate in all team functions; however, redshirt players cannot participate in games. If a player participates in a single game, his or her redshirt status will be void. If a player is classified as a redshirt, he or she is given five years to complete his or her four seasons of on-field eligibility. If a player suffers a season-ending injury before the second half of the season or before he or she competes in three games, the student athlete can petition for a medical hardship with the NCAA. Those who participate in collegiate sports at some point during their career will experience injuries and or illnesses. This may be as simple as a common cold or a minor sprain. When injuries occur, the media and supporters of a college program often discuss the consequences of that injury and speculate about a student athlete's recourses. Phrases such as "medical hardship" and "extension of the five-year clock" (i.e., extension of eligibility, clock extension, etc.) are commonly heard or observed in newspaper articles or other forums. However, they are not the same; medical hardships and extensions of the five-year clock are two distinct concepts, and qualifying for and applying for one entails a process and issues different from the other.

It is valuable for student athletes to comprehend medical hardships and extensions of the five-year clock. In addition, student athletes should be aware that in the Division I level of the NCAA, student athletes have five years within which to participate in four seasons of competition (i.e., a five-year clock). Any level of participation in a competition can trigger the use of a season of competition. If a student athlete redshirts (i.e., does not compete), but is evaluated as healthy, then he or she will be charged a year against the student athlete's five-year clock but not a season of competition. If a student athlete participates in only one contest near the end of the season, but was healthy for the duration of the season of competition, the student athlete has used one season of competition and one year of his or her five-year clock (the five-year clock begins once the student athlete enrolls full-time in a two- or four-year institution and is tolled only in cases of U.S. military service, church missions, and other specifically designated forms of service). What if, during the next two years a student athlete successively incurs season-ending injuries? Does the student athlete qualify for a medical hardship and/or an extension of his or her eligibility? Concerning a medical hardship, the answer depends on the circumstances, but as for an extension, that is the subject of the next section.

A medical hardship can be defined as a form of relief that a university's student athlete will receive after a university's application to the conference only if:

- the student athlete's injury or illness was incapacitating;
- the student athlete's incapacitating injury or illness occurred during the first half of the season and before competition in more than two contests or 20 percent of the season's scheduled contests (whichever is greater); and
- the injury or illness is supported by contemporaneous medical documentation.

If 20 percent of a season is a fraction (e.g., 2.4), the fraction is rounded up to the next whole number. If affirmative, the effect of the medical hardship is that the student athlete's participation does not result in the use of a season of competition; nevertheless, the year that has passed does count against the student athlete's five-year clock.

Some student athletes may be classified as greenshirts. Student athletes identified as greenshirt recruits enroll one semester early and join a Football Bowl Subdivision program for the beginning of the spring semester in January. Normally, greenshirts are expected to participate immediately as a true freshman. With an accelerated transition period, greenshirt student athletes can enroll early and gain valuable exposure, putting them ahead of the learning curve, giving them time to acclimate to campus, participate in spring practice, fully digest an offensive or defensive scheme, and the opportunity to develop in a team's strength and conditioning program. More often than not, greenshirts are among the nation's best prospects at their respective positions, often evaluated by coaches as strong enough, talented enough, and capable to quickly adjust to collegiate athletics and college life.

Student athletes who become grayshirts are recruits who are offered a delayed scholarship. Grayshirts are student athletes who postpone their enrollment until after the conclusion of the upcoming season. Often times grayshirts will take classes, even as part-time students, but do not officially join their identified college or university program until the ensuing spring semester. Collegiate athletic departments use the grayshirt to add additional recruits without sacrificing scholarship numbers. Although a grayshirt graduates along with other prospects from their class, delaying the player's enrollment allows a program to count the grayshirt student athletes scholarship offer toward the following season's total of scholarships offered. Lastly, student athletes classified as blueshirts permit athletic programs to delay a scholarship to the following year. This allows a university to oversign beyond the 25-scholarship limit and play a prospect immediately rather than waiting until the following spring.

Transfers

A student athlete's decision to transfer to another school is an important and often difficult one. Before student athletes act, they should do the research. Student athletes should make sure they understand how transferring will affect them, so they can minimize the negative impact that can occur concerning their education or their chances to participate in collegiate athletics. The NCAA strives to "help make the transition to [the student's] next school a smooth one so [they] may continue [their] education and, at the same time, continue to participate in [their] sport. But [they] have a responsibility in this process as well." They need to learn as much as they can to protect their own eligibility.

Steps to Take Before a Student Athlete Transfers

1. Select which school is right for you. Your school choice should help you satisfy both your academic and athletic goals.
2. Acquire information that helps you understand the transfer and eligibility rules for the NCAA, your new conference, and the school you plan to join. When you begin to think about going to a new school, understand that the rules are different depending on whether you want to transfer to an NCAA Division I, II, or III school, and whether you are currently enrolled at a two-year or a four-year school. In some cases, conference rules can be more restrictive than NCAA rules.
3. Make certain you speak with individuals such as a coach, advisor, or admissions counselor at the school you are interested in attending to ensure you understand their admission requirements. Before you call, you will more often than not need to get a release form or written permission from your current school to talk to the new school.
4. It is very important that you apply to be admitted to the school you want to attend.

When Can I Compete?

Student athletes who transfer may be required to sit out of competition for a year. Often, this is an NCAA requirement for transferring rules to help student athletes adjust to their new school. Student athletes should seek to work closely with their athletics compliance personnel as they plan the details of their transfer.

Hazing

Hazing in intercollegiate sports is forbidden. However, most college athletes indicate that they have been hazed. The federal government has mandated that allegations of hazing-related sexual assault and sodomy among high school and college sports teams be tracked along with all campus sexual assaults. Hazing is illegal in 44 states, but this has not deterred hazing on college campuses. At the college level, 80 percent of NCAA athletes say they have experienced some form of hazing during their college athletic career, while 42 percent reported a history of also being hazed in high school. Coaches must promote a team culture that develops character and leadership and one that does not tolerate hazing on any level. Hazing is dangerous regardless if an athlete voluntarily participates in hazing rituals. These rituals consist of forcing athletes to participate in drinking games, paddling, excessive exercise, and verbal abuse. These rituals also include forcing student athletes to carry equipment, make prank phone calls, destroy property, and harass people. Some student athletes have been tied up and abandoned, forced to buy food, or forced to commit crimes. Most student athletes do not report hazing because they are not comfortable telling their coaches or athletic directors. Athletes also do not report hazing because they do not believe that the administration would handle the situation correctly and would make it worse. Universities and their athletic programs must take a tough stand on hazing. Those institutions that have fraternities and sororities are more likely to have sports teams that haze.

In 2013, Cornell University suspended its lacrosse program after alcohol-related hazing of freshmen recruits. These hazing incidents involved underage drinking. The team held a party and underclassmen were forced to stand in a circle and drink large amounts of beer. They were bound by a rope that was threaded through their belt loops and many were forced to drink until they vomited. Underclassmen were also forced to do menial tasks for upperclassmen. The team was censured and had to undergo anti-hazing education programs and workshops.

In 2014, the University of New Mexico women's soccer team members were accused of hazing. In this incident, the underclassmen soccer players were made to participate in team hazing and initiation rituals. Team members were blindfolded and brought to a party and made to drink alcohol. The underclassmen were not of legal drinking age. It was also stated that the female student athletes were sprayed with a warm soapy liquid and made to strip naked and then wear silly clothing and were forced to kiss the butt of an upperclassmen. Investigators also found that they were forced to perform inappropriate and suggestive acts on frozen hotdogs. After the incident was resolved, the head soccer coach was suspended and members of the team were found to have violated the university's code of conduct and were sanctioned, which included undergoing diversity training and community service.

It may appear that the members of the soccer team received a very minor punishment. New Mexico is one of six states without anti-hazing laws.

In 2015, St. Olaf College in Minnesota canceled its baseball season due to hazing. The incidents at St. Olaf included underage drinking, displays of servitude, ridicule, and harassment. The upperclassmen forced underclassmen to serve in the cafeteria, and hazing also took place off campus. Moreover, the student athletes attempted to cover up the hazing incidents. University administrators discovered the hazing incidents through social media.

LGBTQ Athletes

Historically, collegiate athletics has been a very hostile environment for those who are not identified as traditional athletes. Transitioning from high school is a scary experience, compounded with decisions concerning one's beliefs, socioeconomic status, and sexual orientation. Many athletes fear coming out because of the potential abuse they think they may face. Collegiate athletics has been forced to become more inclusive in regards to lesbian, bisexual, gay, transgendered, queer, and athletes who question their sexuality or sexual orientation. The NCAA includes gender expression and sexual orientation in its "Inclusion Initiative Framework." The office of inclusion is committed to providing education, policy, and resources that support LGBTQ students and the coaches and administrators who educate and lead them in athletics departments. This office has taken the lead in forming the best practices in inclusiveness measures. The NCAA provides information about the definitions and terminology about sexual orientation.

Even with the NCAA's focus on inclusiveness, there are still discriminatory practices that have been exercised by some sports programs and coaches. Female coaches thought to be bisexual or lesbian are harassed, stereotyped, fired, or targeted for negative recruiting by rival coaches. Within women's sports, rival athletic programs will imply that coaches or athletes on a team are lesbians. These kinds of tactics are based on stereotypes and myths and are used as a ploy to gain an advantage in recruiting.

In some cases, a perceived sexual orientation has caused a hostile and offensive environment for a college student athlete. In 2006, a student athlete at Penn State was kicked off of the women's basketball team because her head women's basketball coach believed that she was a lesbian. The coach had a history of discriminating against players she believed were lesbian. The player sued the university and the coach. The lawsuit was settled and the head coach was required to attend diversity training sessions and fined $10,000. In 2014, a Division I basketball player came out as gay. This marked the first time an openly gay male athlete came out while he was still competing in Division I men's basketball. Also in 2014, a football player at University of Missouri came out as gay to the world on ESPN's *Outside the Lines* show. This football player was the Southeastern Conference Defensive Player of the Year and had already been out to his teammates and coaches. The coming-out experiences of these two players were positive because of allies who supported their decision. This included coaches, teammates, and athletic departments.

Gender identity and sexual orientation are not the same things. Transgender people may be straight, gay, lesbian, or bisexual. A person who is transitioning from male to female and is attracted solely to men would identify as a straight woman. The term *transgendered* describes individuals whose gender identity and expression differs from what is associated, typically, with their sex assigned at birth. Individuals who identify as transsexual or transgender are often those who are born with male or female anatomies, but they feel as though they have been born into the "wrong body." Some transgender individuals take hormones or undergo surgical procedures to modify their bodies to reflect their gender identity. Others transitioning may include changing their names and using pronouns with which they identify. Transitioning may also include wearing clothes and hairstyles that reflect the gender with which they identify.

Very few athletic programs have formally adopted policies regarding transgendered athletes. The NCAA sent recommended guidelines to universities in 2011. Many athletic departments have been slow to adopt policies. Those athletic programs that have adopted policies have varying policies. Most have decided to let transgendered athletes participate based on their expressed gender identities. Most of these policies have been controversial. The Olympics' policy allows a transgendered athlete to compete only after they have had gender reassignment surgery and at least two years of hormone therapy. Kye Allums was the first openly transgender NCAA athlete to play Division I sports. Allums came out when he was playing on the women's basketball team at George Washington University in 2010. Departments and personnel in athletics are responsible for creating, supporting, and maintaining an inclusive and nondiscriminatory environment in their programs. Transgendered athletes are not a new phenomenon in sports.

Educators must address transgender issues in athletics for several reasons. Chief among these reasons is that schools must reflect the value of equality and provide opportunities in sports for students of color, women, students with disabilities, and lesbian, gay, and bisexual students.

Title IX

All universities and their athletic departments are governed by nondiscriminatory policy in compliance with Title IX of the Educational Amendments Act of 1972. Title IX of the Education Amendments Act of 1972 protects people from discrimination on the basis of sex in any federally funded education program or activity. Although this law is better known for protecting student athletes from discrimination in athletics, this law covers entities that receive funding from the federal government. There are three basic areas that athletic departments must comply with to meet the requirements of Title IX. These areas are participation, financial assistance, and treatment.

With participation, there must be sports offered for male and female athletes, and there is a three-pronged test to determine if an athletic department offers male and female student athletes equal opportunity. The university and its athletic department must offer proportionality. If there is a group who is underrepresented, there has to be an equal ratio of male to female athletes in order for a school to be in compliance. The school must also show a history and continuing practice for the underrepresented sex. During the 1970s, many universities began to offer women's sports in order to comply with Title IX. During the 1980s, some universities discontinued sports to equalize opportunities. Universities and their athletic departments are required to effectively accommodate the interests and abilities of their students. Under Title IX, these institutions must provide opportunities for individuals of each sex to participate in sports, as well as provide those individuals with competitive team schedules.

Under Title IX, universities and their athletic departments must provide equal athletic benefits and opportunities for their student athletes. Title IX does not require that each men's and women's team receive exactly the same services and supplies, but it looks at the entirety of the treatment the men's and women's programs receive as a whole. The following are the areas in which universities and their athletic departments must ensure that both male and female athletes receive equal treatment:

- Male and female programs must have equal locker rooms, practice, and competitive facilities.
- Male and female programs must have equal quality and amount of equipment and supplies.
- Male and female programs must have equal practice times and scheduling of games.
- Male and female programs must have equal time and access to promotion by sports information personnel.
- Male and female programs must be in comparable equivalence of qualified full-time and part-time coaches, assistant coaches, and graduate assistants.
- Male and female programs must provide equal access to travel and modes of transportation and daily allowances and dining when traveling.
- Male and female athletes must have equal access to the availability of academic tutoring.
- Male and female athletes must have equal access to medical training facilities and services.
- Male and female athletes must have equal access to housing and dining facilities and other services on campus.
- Male and female sports program coaches must have equal opportunities and resources to recruit student athletes for their programs.

- Male and female sports program support services must include the same amount of administrative, secretarial, and clerical assistance.

While Title IX does not require that athletic programs produce mirror images for male and female sports, it does require equality to opportunity and access. Title IX does not require equal distribution of funds for male and female athletic programs. The only direct dollar-for-dollar requirement is in the area of financial assistance provided for athletics. Title IX requires universities and their athletic departments to spend dollars proportional to participation rates. Therefore, if $600,000 is awarded in athletic scholarships and the participation ratio is an equal split of male to female athletes, $300,000 must be awarded to female athletes and $300,000 must be awarded to male athletes. In other areas, the equality standard is measured by equal opportunity. The penalty for a university and the athletic program not complying with Title IX is to withdraw federal funding from this institution. Most universities are not in full compliance with Title IX, and federal funds have never been pulled from a university for not complying. The Office of Civil Rights is the agency in charge of enforcing Title IX. If the Office of Civil Rights receives a complaint, they are obligated to investigate the claims no matter how minor they may appear. It is important to note that Title IX does not require the reduction of opportunities for male athletes in order to increase opportunities for female athletes. Universities and athletic programs that reduce male sports to comply with Title IX are not honoring the spirit of the law. The spirit of the law is to provide athletic opportunity for female athletes and eliminate poor treatment of female sports programs.

Sexual Violence and Student Athletes

Universities and their athletic departments prohibit sexual violence. Athletics departments are tasked to support campus efforts to prevent cases of sexual assault, harassment, hazing, and abuse. Sexual violence includes rape, sexual assault, sexual battery, and sexual coercion. It is a violation to use manipulation or threats to force someone to perform sexual acts, including sexual touching. Sexual violence includes physical sexual acts perpetrated against a person's will or committed where a person is legally incapable of giving consent. Even if the person agrees but later changes his or her mind, this is interpreted as being sexual violence. Any person can be a committer and any person can be a victim of sexual violence, regardless of their sex, gender, or sexual orientation. State laws often define sexual violence a little differently. In addition to generally violating criminal law, sexual violence seriously interferes with a student's learning and athletic environment. Survivors of sexual assault commonly suffer academically and face depression, post-traumatic stress disorder, and trauma-induced neurobiological changes. They are also more likely to abuse drugs and alcohol and contemplate suicide.

Sexual violence is not about sex. It is about having power over the victim. Although most often sexual violence is committed by men against women, men can be victims and women can be perpetrators of sexual violence. Sexual violence can also occur between members of the same sex, regardless of the sexual orientation of the perpetrator and victim. Sexual violence can happen between people who are dating or married, and having consensual sex in the past does not mean there is automatic consent for future sexual acts.

A story on the *Tennessean* Web site stated that "in 2007, two former Colorado University students who said they had been sexually assaulted reached settlements totaling $2.85 million after they alleged the university created a party culture to show football recruits a 'good time' without proper supervision." The same story reported that in 2016, "a young woman agreed to a $950,000 settlement with Florida State University after she sued over how the school investigated and adjudicated her claim of sexual assault against a prominent football player" (http://www.tennessean.com/story/news/2016/02/09/sweeping-sexual-assault-suit-filed-against-ut/79966450/).

The NCAA and the White House have partnered to stop sexual violence on college campuses. In 2014, President Barack Obama launched the "It's On Us" campaign to end sexual assault on college campuses. All student athletes are urged to take the "It's On Us" pledge. The pledge reads:

I pledge to recognize that non-consensual sex is sexual assault.

I pledge to identify situations in which sexual assault may occur.

I pledge to intervene in situations where consent has not or cannot be given.

I pledge to create an environment in which sexual assault is unacceptable and survivors are supported.

Fewer than 5 percent of sexual assault victims report the incident to law enforcement. Often, survivors face the issues alone. It is probable that college women will face some kind of sexual assault during their academic and student athletic career. Women between the ages 16 and 24 experience sexual assault at rates higher than the rate for all women. Student athletes should seek consent before engaging in any sexual act. Voluntary agreement to engage in sexual contact is the responsibility of both parties to get affirmative, ongoing consent before proceeding. The difference between sex and sexual assault is consent. Consent to sex can always be revoked at any time, even during a sexual act. Consent is needed for each step of the way before engaging in sexual or intimate acts. Drugs and alcohol impair judgment and can contribute to sexual violence. Putting drugs in someone's drink is a crime. Date rape drugs are used to commit sexual violence. Some date rape drugs render their victims helpless and unable to speak. It is best to be proactive. Student athletes should monitor their own drinks. If a student suspects that he or she or another student athlete has been drugged, they should seek medical help and contact the campus police. It is not the survivor's fault, and their use of alcohol or drugs does not make them at fault for sexual violence committed against them.

It is important to remember the following:

- All forms of sexual violence, including rape, sexual assault, sexual battery, and sexual coercion are prohibited.
- Participating in sexual violence can result in suspension, expulsion, termination of scholarship, legal action, and imprisonment.
- Drugging someone's drink is a serious crime. Keep control of your drinks at all times.
- Student athletes should know that common effects of sexual assault are depression, academic decline, abuse of drugs and alcohol, post-traumatic stress disorder, and contemplation of suicide.
- Student athletes should be honest and open with their friends about sexual assault.
- Do not be a bystander. Intervene in an appropriate way if you see something.
- Student athletes should trust their gut. Understand that if something looks like it could be a negative situation, it probably is.
- Student athletes should be direct. If someone looks like they may need help, ask them if they are alright.
- Ask a friend, resident assistant or community assistant, bartender, or host to step in if you see something and need to get help.
- Student athletes should be cognizant of individuals who have had too much to drink.
- Enlist help from the friends of someone who is too intoxicated to consent to ensure they leave safely.
- Student athletes must recognize and understand the potential dangers of someone who discusses plans to target a possible victim at a party.
- Students athletes should be aware of techniques and practices used to deliberately intoxicate, isolate, or corner someone else.
- Student athletes should understand that if someone does not consent or is incapable of providing consent to sex, it is rape.
- Student athletes should never blame the victim.

Bystanders play an important role in the deterrence of sexual violence and relationship violence. Student athletes who observe violence or witness the conditions that perpetuate violence should report these to the appropriate people. These individuals include coaches, athletic directors, and faculty. Universities should strive to promote and support a culture of community accountability where bystanders actively engage in the prevention of violence without causing further harm.

The Grind

Consider the following narrative from a student athlete blog on the *Huffington Post* Web site:

> When everyone on campus was leaving for summer break, so was I. My summer break was 10 days instead of three months. Just 10 days after finals we began "optional" workouts. What "optional" really means is that you have an option of whether or not you actually want to play this year. Therefore the majority of the team is on campus during the summer working hard and getting ready for the upcoming season. But these "optional" workouts are only the calm before the storm, because fall camp is not optional. Fall camp marks the beginning of a new season and the beginning of the longest three weeks of the year. At any given time during camp approximately 89 percent of the team could not tell you if today was a Monday or a Friday. That's because during camp there are no days off and every day is the same. A camp day goes something like this.
>
> You wake up at 7:00 A.M. to get ready for meetings at 7:30 A.M. Watching cartoons in the morning is fun, but for some reason watching film of last night's practice in the morning doesn't seem to be as attractive. After fighting sleep for a little over an hour it's time to head over to the stadium for the first practice of the day. After two and half hours on the field it's off to lunch.
>
> For a lot of the guys on the team, outside of dinner, lunch is the highlight of the day. Lunch is a time when everyone gets to eat which a lot of guys on the team really seem to enjoy.
>
> After lunch there are position meetings at 3:30 P.M. At meetings we take a look at the film of the practice we just had only a few hours earlier. After another hour of film, it's time to get a lift in. After lifting weights for a little over an hour it's time for dinner, which besides lunch is the highlight of the day for a lot of guys.
>
> After dinner there are more meetings. After meetings there is more practice. Now that all football related activities are finally done for the day it's time to get some sleep, wake up in the morning and do the same thing again tomorrow.
>
> During camp, football is a full-time job. When school starts, that doesn't change. There are fewer hours spent on the field, but those hours are now committed toward the classroom. Regrettably I can tell you from firsthand experience that balancing your sport with your schoolwork is no simple task.
>
> Because of our football schedule we cannot take any classes after 2:00 P.M. And after practice finishes at around 7:00 P.M., catching up with schoolwork isn't always the first thing on your mind. Traveling every other weekend can cause you to miss out on class time and a social life.
>
> Being a student athlete is a full-time job; it's not easy.

Harassment and a Hostile Environment

Harassment is a form of discrimination that violates Title VII of the Civil Rights Act of 1964 and defined as unwelcomed "conduct based on race, color, religion, sex, including pregnancy, national origin, or genetic information." Harassment is unlawful. Some important points to understand about harassment are the following:

- Enduring the offensive behavior unlawfully becomes a condition of continued participation in athletics.
- It creates an environment as a result of severe or pervasive conduct that a reasonable person would consider intimidating, hostile, or abusive.
- Those who file a discrimination charge, testify, or participation in an investigation, proceeding, or lawsuit are protected from retaliation by anti-discrimination laws.

Snubs, annoyances, irritations, and isolated incidents are not considered harassment unless they rise to a severe level. Offensive conduct may include but is not limited to offensive jokes, slurs, epithets, name calling, physical assaults, threats, ridicule, mockery, offensive objects, or photographs. The victim does not have to be the person harassed. It can be anyone who is offended or affected by the offensive conduct. Quid pro quo harassment occurs in the workplace if an authority figure such as a coach athletic director, administrator, or faculty member offers or hints that she will give the student athlete something in return for satisfaction of a sexual demand. This also occurs when an authority figure says he or she will not reprimand a student athlete in exchange for some type of sexual exchange. For example, a coach cannot demand a sexual favor for a student athlete to keep their scholarship or to receive more playing time. Repeated advances can lead to creating a hostile work environment.

A hostile environment is created when a person feels uncomfortable or scared to be in a certain space due to offensive behavior, intimidation, or abuse by people in that space. To determine whether an environment is hostile, the Equal Employment Opportunity Commission looks at certain factors such as:

- the number of individuals involved and the degree to which the conduct affected education;
- the type, frequency, duration, location, and context of the conduct;
- the age and sex of the alleged harasser and the subject or subjects of the harassment; and
- the nature of the conduct and whether the conduct is gender-based.

Times have changed in collegiate athletics. The NCAA and university athletic departments are cracking down on sexual harassment in collegiate sports. Any charges and claims are being taken very seriously and student athletes found guilty of these sorts of violations are being prosecuted to the full extent of the law. It is imperative that all student athletes become aware of the consequences of sexual misconduct and of creating a hostile environment for their teammates and student athletes in other sports.

SUGGESTED READINGS

Byers, Walter, with Charles Hammer. *Unsportsmanlike Conduct: Exploiting College Athletes.* Ann Arbor: University of Michigan Press, 1995.

Coakley, Jay. *Sports in Society: Issues and Controversies.* Boston: McGraw-Hill, 2004.

Hawkins, Billy, Joseph Cooper, Akilah Carter-Francique, and J. Kenyatta Cavil, eds. *The Athletic Experience at Historically Black Colleges and Universities: Past, Present and Persistence.* Lanham, MD: Rowman & Littlefield, 2015.

Smith, Ronald A. *Pay for Play: A History of Big-Time College Athletic Reform.* Urbana: University of Illinois Press, 2010.

Suggs, Welch. *A Place on the Team: The Triumph and Tragedy of Title IX.* Princeton, NJ: Princeton University Press, 2006.

PART V

Balancing Athletics and Academics in College

STEP TEN: SUPPORTING SUCCESSFUL ACADEMIC HABITS

Counseling and Academic Advisors

Most university athletic departments have counseling and advisement centers that provide counseling services with professional counselors who listen and are concerned about student athletes' mental health needs. These counseling professionals listen and attempt to make students' college experience productive and rewarding. Athletes use the counseling centers that are available for other students. Counseling centers offer numerous programs to assist students adjust to college and any other problems they may be experiencing. They usually provide crisis and psychological counseling to students who need these services. These services are designed to help students overcome any obstacles to life goals or traumatic situations through customary methods of problem solving and traditional counseling. In the case of extreme psychological problems, most universities have either an on-campus psychologist or they have contracts with mental health professionals in the community to offer assistance. University counseling centers help students learn how to cope with their personal problems and assist students with other behaviors such as building communication skills, developing assertiveness, developing test-taking skills, time management, and building stress-coping mechanisms. University counselors also assist students working through difficult situations such as sexual assault, relationship abuse, date rape, HIV and AIDS, and alcohol and drug abuse. University counselors help students with personal growth through individual and group counseling sessions that provide opportunities for students to participate with peers and professionals in exploring feelings, behaviors, and other common concerns in a supportive atmosphere and to gain clarification and feedback. These counseling sessions allow students to develop a plan of appropriate action. Ultimately, a university counseling center's mission is to help students learn to cope, identify choices, make better decisions, and turn problems into learning experiences.

Most athletic departments offer their own academic advisors, who assist students in selecting the correct courses for their majors and assist students in keeping on track for degree completion and graduation. Universities have different policies and procedures that address many of the more difficult questions that a student may have. Universities usually have academic advising and academic services as well as the university counseling center to address specific questions such as:

How do I drop a course?

When can I drop a course?

How do I go about dropping a course?

How can I add a class?

How do I withdraw from the university?

How do I preregister?

Where can I go to discuss my academic difficulties?

Where can I go for academic advice?

What if I just don't know what to do with my future?

With whom can I talk if I'm not sure what to major in?

How do I change my major?

Who can help me improve my study habits?

Where can I go for tutoring?

A university's counseling center and the academic advisement center are fantastic on-campus resources for student athletes.

Academic Calendar

Many universities operate under either a "semester" or a "quarter" system. These may also be called "terms." Generally, academic years are divided in two periods. The fall term usually begins in August or September for most schools and spring term usually begins in January. Semesters can last from 12 to 20 weeks. Under the semester system summer terms usually have a shorter number of weeks. Under a quarter system, there are four grading periods that are treated equally. Quarters are usually 12 weeks and are the equivalent of two 18-week semesters. Each university has an academic calendar that is set by the university registrar in consultation with administrators and other units on campus. The academic calendar lays out all of the important dates during an academic semester or quarter. These dates usually include the registration period, the opening day of classes, midterm and final exam schedules, and all breaks that will occur during the academic year. This calendar also lays out when grades are due, and special events such as convocations and graduations.

Syllabus

A syllabus is an outline of the topics being covered in a course. The plural form of the word syllabus is syllabi. Professors will usually hand out a syllabus on the first day of class. In most cases, before a course begins, the only information that a student may have about a course is the information found in the course catalog. The syllabus functions as a guide throughout the course in which students are enrolled. It provides more specific information than a catalog. In the syllabus the professor provides the conception of the course, assignments, examinations, due dates, the grading scale for the course, and other pertinent information about their expectations for the course. It also gives the student the structure of how the course will be taught and how examinations will be structured, e.g., multiple choice, short answer, essay, or a combination. In the syllabus, the professor provides all of the course policies, which can pertain to attendance and missed assignments. The consequences of violating policies are also provided in the syllabus. The syllabus usually contains a list of tentative dates of readings and when examinations and assignments are due. The most prominent mistakes students make regarding the syllabus is losing the syllabus and failing to obtain another copy, or failing to keep up with the assigned readings. Sometimes due dates on a syllabus may change depending on the flow of a class discussion or other circumstances that interrupt the pace of teaching and learning in a class. The syllabus can be viewed as a contract with both parties; the student and professor agree to uphold the contract. The syllabus is not written in stone, but the only person who can change the syllabus is the professor. A syllabus also provides students with an indication of a professor's personality and how tough they may be in instructing the course. The professors sometimes come across extra tough in their syllabus in an effort to scare off students who are not serious about the class. Some students who do not want to work really hard may use the drop/add process to change classes to avoid difficult or stern professors.

Dropping and Adding Courses

Every university has a procedure called the drop and add process. This procedure may differ from university to university, but the principle of allowing students to change their schedule underlies the process. This process may be completed by using a paper form or online depending on the university. Usually during the first 10 days, students are allowed to add courses to their schedule or switch times and days of classes to the schedule. At most universities, students may drop or add classes for the first 10 days of a semester but after the 10th day of the semester, students may only drop courses. Only in exceptional circumstances are students allowed to add courses after the official drop and add period ends. Any addition after the end of the official drop and add period usually requires permission from the professor, dean, and registrar. Any changes to a student's schedule should be approved by an academic advisor or a faculty advisor. In general, a course dropped during the first four weeks of classes is not entered on the student's record. At most universities, students are responsible for the accuracy of their registration and any changes that they make to their schedules. Students should keep up with the accuracy of their course schedules through their university Web accounts.

Midterm and Final Exams

Midterm examinations are exams given at the midpoint of a semester. These exams are given to students to assess their knowledge of course material up to the middle of the semester. Dates for midterms are determined prior to the semester and are usually listed in the professor's syllabus that is distributed during the first week of class. In some cases, the midterm exam can be up to 50 percent of a student's overall semester grade. The actual exam may be objective—multiple choice, matching, and true or false questions—or they may be subjective—essay, short answer, or oral interviews. Some exams may be a mixed-form exam using both objective and subjective methods, where the first part may be multiple choice and the second part may consist of three or four essay questions. Final exams are given at the end of a semester and test a student's knowledge of course material over the entire semester. Like midterm examinations, a professor may use subjective, objective, or mixed-method exams. In some cases, a professor may choose to only test students on information covered since the midterm exam. Depending on a professor's discretion, exams can count as a large portion of a student's overall semester grade and therefore become a source of great stress during midterm and final exam periods.

Academic Status

One of the most important aspects of college is establishing a good grade point average (GPA). A student's GPA is determined by the grades that they receive in individual courses and are tabulated over time. In general, a cumulative GPA is determined by dividing the total number of points earned by the total number of grades or hours passed satisfactorily. Grade point values per semester hour of credit differ slightly depending on the school. Some universities use a plus/minus system in grading. If students maintain exceptional academic standing and an excellent GPA, they may receive specific designated honors such as cum laude, magna cum laude, and summa cum laude. If students fail courses, they may be placed on academic warning, academic probation, or academic suspension. When a student is placed on academic probation, their GPA has fallen under a 1.00 for a particular term. If a student's cumulative GPA has fallen below a 2.00, then they may be placed on academic warning. Students placed on academic warning may not enroll for more than 12 hours. By taking a limited number of hours, students should be able to improve their grades and avoid being placed on academic probation or academic suspension. Usually students placed on academic probation are also limited in the number of hours they may enroll. A student on academic probation must achieve at least a 2.00 GPA each grading period; until this academic standing is reached, they could be academically suspended. After a student has been placed on academic suspension, the student will have to reapply to be readmitted into the university and meet the conditions defined under the suspension.

Transferring

On occasion students may find that they may want or need to transfer to another university. There are many reasons why students may transfer from one university to another. Some students experience social or financial problems, which may lead to a decision to transfer. Some students may have trouble adjusting to being away from home. Some students may realize that the school that they presently attend was not the right choice for them. Some students may not like the climate or the city where their university is located. For some students, they may not like the food, residence hall, or their roommate. Other reasons students transfer include the need for spiritual enlightenment or political consciousness, and finding their identity. Each academic year there are many students who transfer or consider transferring, so students should not be ashamed if they are considering transferring.

There are many factors that students should consider when making the decision to transfer. Students should determine why they want to transfer. They must determine if it would be an advantage or disadvantage to transfer. Weighing the pros and cons about transferring will assist students in making the right decision for them. After deciding that transferring is the best option, there are several things that must take place such as researching potential four-year universities or if a two-year school may be a better option. It is routine for students to transfer from a two-year college to a four-year university. However, there are instances where students transfer from a four-year institution to a two-year institution. Students may also want to consider if they will lose credits by transferring and if the university being considered offers the same major or a newly chosen major. When transferring to another university, students must present their college transcripts and in some cases their high school transcripts as well. The presentation of high school transcripts usually depends how many hours the student has completed in college.

Generally, the grade of "C" is the lowest course grade that is acceptable in a transfer. Some universities will sometimes accept a C- or D grades if the transfer student is from a university in their higher education system. Usually, remedial or development courses are not transferable. It is often difficult for transferring students to find on-campus housing so it is best to do this early in the transfer process. Students should make sure that transferring does not become a pattern of moving from university to university. Students should also make sure that they have a solid plan of how a transfer fits into their long-term plans because a degree will be harder to obtain if there is not a plan for their academic career.

Contact Hours and Course Load

Contact hours are the amount of hours that a student is actually in class receiving instruction. *Contact hours* and *credit hours* are terms that are closely related. Credit hours are the amount of hours that students are given credit for receiving a passing grade in a course. The credit hour can differ for the amount of contact hours that a student has for a class. Typically, credit hours range from 3 credit hours up to 12 credit hours. The typical number of credit hours for one class is 3 credit hours. There are a certain number of credit hours needed to receive a degree. Each school defines the total number and types of credits necessary for degree completion, with every course being assigned a value in terms of credits. The number of credit hours taken builds a student's course load. *Course load* is the number of courses or credits a student takes during a specific semester. Students may be asked the question, "How many hours are you are taking this semester?" The student is being asked about the total number of credit hours a student is taking during a particular semester.

Faculty members are required to hold office hours. Office hours are the hours of the day that professors are in their offices so that students can go and ask for assistance. Office hours are underutilized by most students. Professors expect students to use their judgment to decide when to come for office hours. Professors usually announce their office hours during first few sessions of classes. On Web-based courses, office hours are also posted on the first few sessions of the course opening. During online courses, office hours may be conducted through chat functions, Skype, or telephone.

Students are classified into either full-time or part-time student status. Full-time students are those students enrolled in at least 12 credit hours of courses.

Probation, Suspension, and Readmission

Students who do not meet the normal standards of progress may be placed on probation. When a student is placed on probation, restrictions are placed on the student. These restrictions may consist of limiting both the number of courses in which a student may enroll and extracurricular activity involvement. Academic probation is a notification that a student's performance falls below a university's requirement for good academic standing. Students can avoid academic probation by keeping a GPA above 2.0. At some universities, a student can be placed on academic probation because they have withdrawn from too many courses during a given semester. Standards for probation may be different depending on the policies set by the university. These requirements can be found in the university catalog. If a student is on probation and their grades fall below the required GPA, a student may face suspension from a university. At most colleges, if students are suspended they will have to sit out for a designated time. This designated time can be from one semester to two semesters. If a student is suspended, they must apply for readmission before they can enroll in classes again. When students apply for readmission from suspension, there is not a guarantee that students will be readmitted. The process varies depending on the university, but a student usually has to meet with an advisor or go before a committee to gain reentry. Once students gain readmittance, they may have to meet certain requirements or conditions such as not enrolling over a certain number of hours or keeping a certain GPA.

During a student's college career, they may need to withdraw from school. Withdrawal means that a student drops all courses during a current semester. Universities have a process that students must follow to be officially withdrawn from their classes. Simply choosing to not attend classes is not withdrawing from school. During a semester, a student may want to withdraw if there is an emergency, serious illness, or military duty. A student's financial aid may be affected if they choose to withdraw. A student's federal aid is awarded based on the percentage of time enrolled in courses for the semester. Contingent upon the date of withdrawal, student aid will be adjusted according to the federal Return of Title IV Funds formula. Based on the effective date of withdrawal, any federal aid received during the semester will be subject to the federal return calculation. The last documented date of attendance will be recognized as the student's withdrawal date. The instructors of courses will determine the withdrawal date. The grace period prior to repayment begins when a student withdraws.

The Perkins Loan grants a nine-month grace period and Federal Stafford Loans grant a six-month grace period. Students who re-enroll before the end of a grace period will be granted a new grace period upon leaving school. Otherwise, the student will need to request a loan deferment when he or she re-enrolls. Some students may choose to drop out of college. Dropping out of college is enrolling in college with the intent of pursuing a degree and then failing to complete a college education. People drop out for many reasons, and just because people drop out of college does not mean that they cannot become successful. If a student chooses to drop out of college, they should make sure that they have a career plan to pursue. While some students drop out, others may stop out. To stop out is to withdraw temporarily from higher education or employment in order to pursue another activity. With the rising cost of college, it is not so uncommon for students to stop and then return to continue pursuit of their degrees. Just as dropping out, students should have plans in place to determine how they will return to school after stopping out. After dropping out and stopping out, many students drift away from pursuing college education and never return.

Study Halls

The purpose of study hall is to provide a structured approach to studying for student athletes. For most student athletes, study hall is mandatory. Study hall sessions are monitored by academic support personnel in the department of athletics.

Sometimes coaches monitor student athletes. Student athletes who participate in study halls are expected to bring all materials necessary to complete assignments or studying. Though the number of hours required for study halls vary from university to university, most schools require at least six hours per week in study hall for student athletes. Some universities use a sliding scale consisting of the number of credit hours enrolled, GPA, and classification. At most institutions, walk-in tutoring is also available. There are usually tutors who are available to tutor student athletes in general subjects such as English, history, and math. Most athletic departments make student athletes take an orientation course that teaches about issues and life as a college student athlete. They examine issues such as NCAA eligibility requirements and general campus knowledge. Most athletic departments use progress reports to monitor a student athlete's progress and attendance. This information is gathered to make sure student athletes are attending classes and are passing the courses in which they are enrolled. If there is a problem with attendance or academic performance, usually a meeting is scheduled with the academic athletic support services and with the appropriate coaches to review and rectify problems with a student athlete's poor academic performance. Most athletic departments apply general rules like these below to govern behavior during study hall hours:

1. Do not disturb other student athletes who are studying.
2. Laptops are usually permitted, but only for academic assistance.
3. Proper attire must be worn; no stocking caps, hats, or do-rags, etc.
4. No food is permitted in study hall.
5. Cell phones or text messaging are not permitted in study hall.
6. Falsifying hours spent in study hall is prohibited.
7. No sleeping at any time.

STEP ELEVEN: MAKING THE GRADES AND ACADEMIC SUCCESS

College orientation is an overall introduction to the university that a student has chosen to attend. When students have reached the orientation stage, they are officially a college student, and orientation is the first step in actual college experience. College orientation usually lasts about two days; however, some colleges also sponsor one-day orientations that are also called drive-in orientations. Before attending orientation the student should read information that the university sends them about the activities that will take place during the orientation session. Since there are multiple orientation sessions, students must make sure that they are showing up on the correct dates. These events usually occur over one to three session periods and give incoming freshmen and transfer students an idea of what to expect as a college student at their university. Orientations are filled with academic and nonacademic activities. Orientations provide incoming students with an opportunity to see the campus, visit resident halls, and meet academic advisors, professors, and department chairs. Most college orientations are aimed at the entire family and are filled with activities for parents accompanying incoming or transfer students. At the conclusion of the orientation session, students usually receive their class schedules for the upcoming semester. While orientation may appear to be fun and games, students must remember that this is the official beginning of their college career.

The First-Year Experience

The first-year experience is a form of an extended orientation for new students at colleges to help them transition from high school to the university setting. Some of these programs last a few weeks while others extend to an entire semester. While the transition experience is unique for each student, first-year experience programs are designed to help all students get comfortable with their new surroundings and connect with the university. These programs are aimed at incoming students and also are an attempt to build community within the university. By offering activities through a concentrated first-year experience that connects students with their universities through targeted programming, universities believe that students are more likely to return for the sophomore year. Some colleges even offer college credit for completing the first-year experience program. Student athletes should take advantage of the first-year experience in order to avoid the isolation that can sometimes be experienced on some college campuses. Depending on the campus, the first-year experience may also provide referral services to students about academic and personal areas and conduct exit interviews for students contemplating withdrawal from the university. They may also act as an emergency contact for students experiencing immediate health or personal problems that may affect their academic performance and class attendance.

There are steps that one can take as a first-year student in college. Student athletes should be patient. This is a new experience, and they will not master every aspect of university life quickly. The campus atmosphere will be new, and this may be overwhelming for some students, but as soon as they become more familiar with the campus and the people that they meet, they will become more comfortable with navigating their new surroundings. It is important to connect with other students on campus. If students talk with fellow students, they will discover that they have similar questions. Professors, counselors, academic advisors, and resident assistants are equipped to help solve problems and direct students to appropriate resources where they may find the answers. There are also numerous offices and programs on university campuses created to enhance students' college experience. Often, these resources go underutilized. Students should take advantage of the many sources of support such as counseling centers, career centers, financial aid programs, mentoring/tutoring programs, diversity offices, and academic advising offices. Student athletes should get involved in various activities on campus. Some student athletes only get involved with activities and events that they believe are directed at student athletes.

While in college, student athletes must not neglect their own needs. They must take time to develop themselves and their talents. This begins with making sure they follow habits of good nutrition, regular exercise, and adequate sleep. Students should not overdo it with extracurricular activities, and they must find a balance between academics and extracurricular activities and hobbies. Students should use their alone time to get to know themselves. A student's time at college should be viewed as an opportunity to develop independence and to learn to take care of their own physical and emotional needs. Students should avoid merely vegetating or becoming a couch potato. Students should not passively deal with any situation that they might encounter; they should deal with their situations actively. Recognize that there are many creative and enjoyable ways to use their time in college. Student athletes must explore opportunities and engage in various activities. Students should not predetermine if they are going to dislike activities prior to engaging in them. Keep an open mind about all activities that take place on campus. They should remember it is okay to explore activities by themselves that people usually do alone like attending sporting events, a movie, or play at a local theater. Student athletes must recognize that their college years should be a period of growth and self-development.

Students should remember to maintain a healthy lifestyle. Students should maintain a balance and take the necessary steps to make sure they eat healthy, get the proper rest, while balancing socializing and other extracurricular activities. Most university campuses have a recreation center, and this can be instrumental in assisting students in alleviating the stress associated with being a college student. The campus recreational center usually provides programs that promote healthy practices and various health topics.

Living in a Residence Hall

Student athletes who move to campus may experience a culture shock. Living away from their parents for the first time may be a very exciting time, but living away from one's parents and assuming more responsibility may also be a frightening and challenging task. Living in a residence hall can be a new and exhilarating experience. Building a community in a residence hall is important, as is establishing ground rules with a roommate or roommates. Some of the typical disputes between roommates arise over room cleanliness, noise complaints, and personality clashes. In most residential hall living facilities, resident assistants, usually second- or third-year students, are responsible for providing leadership for various areas in the living facilities. Students should establish roommate agreements to help guide behaviors and actions while residing in the same living area. Items that could be listed in the roommate agreement include rules for entertaining visitors, personal space, use of each other's items, and privacy. Students' social skills and getting accustomed to living with others must be learned if students are going to be happy living in a residential hall. Living in a residence hall can be a big adjustment for students who are used to their own living space and not used to having to share with others. Many factors contribute to the relationship between roommates; family background, personality traits, and cultural beliefs are some of the major factors. Recognizing these factors may assist students in establishing a good relationship with their roommate. Learning to live with a new roommate can be one of the most challenging aspects of going to college. Roommates having different living habits and lifestyles are the most common source of roommate conflict. Failure to communicate expectations with their roommates about living together can lead to tension and an unbearable living arrangement. During a conflict with a roommate, they should communicate their needs and expectations respectfully. They should also take ownership of their contributions to the conflict.

Disputes between roommates will arise. When there are disputes, how should roommate settle the disputes? There are proper ways in settling roommate disputes. When issues with one's roommate begin to distract from a student's studies and day-to-day living environment, it is then time to attempt to resolve the problem. Settling disputes with roommates may call for mediation by a third party. Residence assistants are trained in handling these situations and have had live simulations of possible scenarios in settling minor roommate disputes. Below are a few suggestions in settling a dispute between roommates calling for the intervention of a resident assistant:

- Be patient and live by the Golden Rule. Do unto others, as you would have them do unto you.
- Privately approach your roommate with issues.
- Keep calm and express the key issues that may be causing problems.
- Try to settle the dispute on your own. If this cannot be accomplished, then seek out your resident assistant.
- Know your resident assistants' on-duty hours. Residence assistants are full-time students and some even hold other part-time jobs, so they may not always be available.
- When a student feels threatened, it may warrant a room change.
- Communication is the key.

In living in residential housing spaces, theft also may be an occurrence. In order to avoid thefts, students should remember to always close and lock their doors when they leave their rooms and keep personal belongings out of sight and in a safe place. Students should lock their doors even if they go down the hall or to the bathroom. If property is stolen, contact the campus police and complete a police report.

During their time in college, students will gain new friends and friendships. Some of these friendships will last a lifetime, others will not. There are a number of ways to meet new friends on campus. Students can meet people (who can become friends) while doing ordinary things during the course of their daily routines. Student athletes should look for ways to get involved with other people and develop friendships. For example, they can:

sit with various people in the cafeteria during lunch and dinner;

change where they sit in class;

find a study partner; or

discover an exercise partner.

Student athletes must put themselves in situations where they will meet new people. If they engage in activities, especially those that they are passionate about, they will likely meet like-minded people and develop friendships. Students should allow friendships to develop naturally. Close friendships develop over time. Usually people begin to share their inner feelings after they have developed trust; therefore it is not a reasonable expectation to expect people that they just meet to share feelings quickly. Clubs, churches, part-time jobs, and volunteer work are great opportunities to meet new people and make new friends. Most important, student athletes should work at developing their social skills and expanding their network of friends.

Personal Safety

All students contribute to making sure their campuses are safe spaces. There are some effective strategies that students should employ to help them remain safe while on campus. Students should use good judgment and trust their instincts. Students should also use common sense. Students should avoid being alone with someone whom they do not know. They should always let someone know where they will be going and the person or people that will be accompanying them. When possible, students should travel in groups and travel in well-lit areas. Students should not leave backpacks, books, purses, or personal property unattended. When possible, students should use their university's transit system. Last, students should avoid using alcohol and drugs because they impair good judgment and big mistakes can occur while intoxicated.

First-Generation Students

First-generation students are classified as students who are the first in their immediate family to attend college. Students who do not have a parent with a college degree often do not perform as well as students who do. Usually, first-generation college students come from families with low incomes or middle-class families without a tradition of its family members attending college. First-generation college students tend to lag behind in graduation rates and grades as those students with parents who have degrees. On college campuses, first-generation students may find it difficult to fit in and sometimes find it difficult to grasp the university language and lingo. First-generation college students may have to rely on additional resources to navigate through college. They may need to rely on advisors and professors for advice more than those who are second- and third-generation college students. As a first-generation college student, it is important to identify their interests and abilities; this will allow them to choose a major that fits their passions and interests. First-generation college students should find upperclassmen or college graduates who were also first-generation, to discuss their college experiences with them. By discussing these experiences, first-generation students gain insightful and impactful knowledge of how to navigate college and gain knowledge of the norms, rules, and expectations of college in order to avoid the pitfalls that can get students off course. These discussions may assist students in developing a support system and keep first-generation students from feeling lost while they are enrolled in college and pursuing their degree. Being a first-generation college student may pose a challenge if there is a lack of family support in terms of advice and understanding of what the student is experiencing. Student athletes find this particularly challenging, as their family and friends who did not go to college may treat them differently when they visit home. Their parents will most likely be supportive. However, their siblings and friends may comment on how much "you have changed." Some may be so blunt as to state "You think you are better than me now."

Extracurricular Activities

Participation in extracurricular activities benefits African American students and those from low socioeconomic backgrounds because these activities usually help African American students connect to a university. It is important not to underestimate the importance of extracurricular activities in the college experience, but it is also important that extracurricular activities are not the most important aspect of a student's college experience. On most university campuses, there are various extracurricular activities that are offered. These activities range from clubs and organizations to intramural sports; students may find a several activities to get involved with on campus. For most African American students and students of color, most college campuses have an organization called the Black Student Association (BSA). This organization and those like it were established to promote a better scholastic, cultural, political, and social life for the African American student at universities. Many students also get involved with the Student Government Association (SGA) or serve on other department or university committees. On most campuses, the SGA is recognized as the representative entity for the student body and involves students who may have questions, ideas, and suggestions for the betterment of the university as a whole. By gaining experience with student government or serving on a committee, African American students can gain better insight into how the university functions and the governing policies and procedures. By becoming a leader in organizations such as fraternities, sororities, clubs, teams, and choirs, students can gain important leadership skills. It also shows a student's dedication, balance, and leadership. Some African American students find it difficult to balance academic and extracurricular activities. They forget to prioritize their activities and extracurricular activities.

becoming consumed with their extracurricular activities instead of their studies. It can be difficult for students to determine if they are involved in too many activities, but students should ask themselves these questions in determining if they are:

1. Do I have enough time to keep up with my readings for classes and complete assignments?
2. Can I get the proper amount of hours of sleep at night (8 hours)?
3. Can I still hang out with my friends on occasion?
4. Can I still make time to talk with my family and friends on occasion?
5. Am I making failing grades on exams and assignments?

One of the biggest mistakes that an African American student athlete can make is to let extracurricular activities take priority over their academics. Learning time management and preventing procrastination will greatly help students balance their academic activities and extracurricular activities.

Academic Culture

The academic culture of a university is extremely important. It is important for students to understand this culture. It is often the case that students have the intelligence and the will to graduate, but sometimes they lack the ability to navigate the academic culture, which causes them to fail in a university setting. Frankly, many students penalize themselves by not exercising the proper etiquette in a classroom and knowing how to properly conduct themselves in a college classroom setting. An academic culture is an atmosphere where faculty and students are intellectually curious about a variety of topics and subjects. It is an atmosphere where faculty and students think critically and beyond what is obvious. The atmosphere in a college classroom is one where ideas are examined and discussed and arguments are supported by facts. It is an atmosphere of self-discovery and where students are evaluated by their professors who are experts in the courses that they are teaching.

Within a university there is an academic culture and it has its own language, assumptions, and acceptable behaviors. Each university has a set of rules, protocols, and traditions. Some rules, protocols, and traditions are universal to college and some are specific to the university that a student attends. If students are to be successful they should honor the rules, protocols, and traditions if they aim to be successful in the academic setting. The language, assumptions, and acceptable behaviors may vary from university to university, but for the most part there are some universal principles expected in an academic setting. It is important for students to know what is acceptable and unacceptable at the university that they attend. Mastering and understanding an academic culture will make their time in college enjoyable and less frustrating and improves a student's chances of graduating. In the classroom, students should come to class early. If a class is in the classroom in which their class is to meet, students should remain quiet outside of the classroom until the professor has dismissed class. Students should not enter the classroom until the professor using the classroom has finished packing up or until they state that it is okay to enter the classroom.

College Classroom Etiquette and Positive Interactions with Professors

There are some behaviors that are unacceptable in a college classroom setting. Students should attend all classes and should not be late to class. Coming to class late is an unnecessary interruption to the professor's lecture. Chronic tardiness shows a professor that a student may be uninterested in learning and taking their college education seriously. Students should use decorum in dealing with their professors. Students should treat their professor like they are their future boss. Students must take ownership of their actions. When they make mistakes, students should be honest with their professors and admit their error. Professors have much more respect for students who admit their mistakes; however, these mistakes cannot be everyday occurrences.

Students must remember to not use unprofessional communication with their professor such as profanities. Often students will use profanities in a classroom discussion; this is not the norm. Even if their professors use profanity while teaching and during class discussions, students should not use profanity in a class setting. Students should listen intently to lectures and participate in all activities during the class. Students should read the syllabus. On the first day that a class meets, the professor will read the syllabus for the course and discuss any questions that students may have. This is the time to get any clarification about assignments or rules of the class. Students miss valuable lessons by not paying attention to the syllabus. There is an old saying, "There are not any stupid questions." Yes, there are stupid questions, especially if they can be found in the professor's syllabus for a course. Students should check the syllabus first before asking questions about readings or assignments. By asking questions that are clearly in the syllabus, it may indicate that a student may not be totally invested in the course. Professors usually take notice of those students who engage in learning during their teaching. Students discredit themselves by looking disinterested by slumping in chairs, sleeping during a class, or using a smart phone. Professors can serve as a wonderful resource for students especially when students need recommendations.

Some college students fear their professors because they do not view them as approachable, and this may be particularly intimidating for student athletes who have had little or no interaction with people of other races. Most professors want all students to view their classes as interesting and they want students to have a genuine interest in the courses that they instruct. Professors are human beings and they are susceptible to the same emotions and feelings as others. With this in mind, professors sometimes make judgments based on assumptions. The way a student interacts with professors and performs on assignments may correctly or incorrectly feed into this judgment. Students should be conscious of how they are perceived on campus. Many professors read the student newspaper and make note of stories about students. Some professors are members of various social media outlets, so do not put questionable or embarrassing information on social media. This is also good advice even after graduation.

Students should remember that professors are not available 24 hours a day. Professors have other interests and obligations besides work. Many students e-mail professors during early mornings or during late nights expecting an immediate response. This is not a reasonable expectation of their professor. Students make the assumption that professors know everything and that we have made "A's" in all of our undergraduate and graduate courses. Professors may only be tangentially knowledgeable about subjects that are not their field of expertise. It is also important for students to note that professors are professionals, which constitutes judging all students impartially. Students sometimes misinterpret professors' professionalism and politeness as "softness."

There are a few strategies that will help students have positive interactions with their professors. Honesty is the best policy when dealing with a professor. Students should be honest with their professors in all situations. The professor is more apt to give students a second chance if they are honest. Students should not pack up their things before the class is over, as this is not only rude but a professor might think that they are not truly interested in the class. Students should not take critical feedback personally when a professor returns an assignment or exam. Students should think about how they performed in a class before asking a professor to serve as a reference for them. Students should also notify their professors if they are going to miss class, especially for an extended period of time. Student athletes should buy or rent required textbooks for all classes and stay on top of their studies from the beginning of the semester. Students should also get a dictionary and a thesaurus and use both when constructing papers. These two items will come in handy with writing papers. Students should notify their professors ahead of time if they will have to miss class. One of the most annoying questions for professors is when students ask, "Did I miss anything important?" when absent. Questions like this do not show forethought and may cause a negative encounter with their professor. Here are other tips on what students should avoid when interacting with their professors that may help them have positive interactions:

1. Students should use supplemental instruction, i.e., labs and writing centers. Using labs and other supplemental services improves their papers and assignments. It also shows that they are willing to do extra work to get a good grade.

2. Students should not stare at their laptops or phones during the entire class. This behavior is an indication that they are not paying attention.

3. Students should not say to a professor, "I missed class, can I turn my assignment in late?" This statement indicates to a professor that the student is poor at time management or is not serious about their education.

4. Students should never say, "I don't have a pencil, do you have extra pencils?" This action shows that they are not prepared for class and may not be serious about pursuing a college education.

5. Students should not ask the professor, "Can we get out of class early?" This question may indicate that the class is not a priority and the student is not serious about graduating.

6. Students should never say, "I stayed up all night to get this assignment finished and I just finished before class." This statement shows that they did not put significant time in completing the assignment.

7. Students should not say, "Is this going to be on the exam?" This statement can be very disruptive and show the professor that they do not have a genuine interest in the course.

8. Students should never say, "I took this class for an easy 'A'." This statement is an insult to a professor.

9. Students should not go to a professor during office hours expecting to change a professor's mind about a grade on an assignment or examination.

10. Students should not go to class in pajamas or any other inappropriate dress. Students should view their time at college as preparation for the world of work.

Students must remember that professors are human, and honesty is the best policy when dealing with a professor. Be honest with professors in all situations. The professor is more apt to give students a second chance if they are honest.

Participating in Class Discussions

There is a proper and improper way for student athletes to express themselves during class discussions. The goal of a class discussion is to present and examine course information and elaborate on key points of the information. Class discussions also allow students to ask questions and get clarification about information that may be unclear. By participating in class discussions, students show professors that they are receiving and understanding the information being presented in class. Students should maintain eye contact with the professor during lectures and practice active listening. Eye contact should also be maintained when participating in class discussions with professors and other students. Looking directly but comfortably at the person to whom they are talking helps communicate their genuine interest. A student looking away or staring too intently can be uncomfortable for the other person. Staring at computers, cell phones, or electronic tablets during a lecture is also an indication that they may not have a genuine interest in the course. Students should maintain good body posture while in the class session and engaging in class discussions. When students are engaged in a discussion with professors or fellow students, they should turn toward them. This positioning makes an interaction with an individual feel much more personal than turning away or to the side. Students who exhibit poor posture by slumping down in their desks may give the impression that they are passive, weak, and timid. While participating in class discussions, facial expressions and gestures are just as important as what students are saying during the discussion. Students' expressions should match what they are saying in the discussion. When angry, the most effective way to deliver the information is to speak with a straight, nonsmiling facial expression. On the other hand, if the information being delivered is lighthearted, a big smile and jovial gestures may be appropriate. Students must control the tone of their voices. Students should use a level and even tone of voice in class discussion. Consider the tone, inflection, and volume when speaking to professors and fellow students. This tone should be clear and convincing.

Some may consider some of the things that a student athlete says in class discussions intimidating because they differ from their own worldview, but a well-thought-out response is much better than a poorly thought-out one. It is probably best to respond in the moment during a class discussion. However, it is also okay to think about a topic or an issue brought up in a class discussion and return to a person at a later time to share thoughts about an issue. Self-discovery and revelation are cornerstones of higher education and the university experience. Most important, practice active listening in all class discussions. Listening reflects a commitment to learning and understanding the information presented in a course. During class discussions, student athletes should attempt to provide content in a manner that allows classmates to not only hear them, but also more likely receive the information. In some courses, discussions may turn to controversial racial topics. Some students who may not have had close interactions with student athletes may say things that they do not agree with and even make them angry during these discussions. During these times, some student athletes may choose not to express their views on these topics for fear that what they say in a discussion may be misconstrued. Other student athletes may express themselves. If students choose to express themselves and their feelings, they should make sure that they use tact and well-thought-out responses during these discussions while challenging their classmates. They must avoid putting students down while expressing views; students do not need to put someone else down to express themselves. It is okay to feel uncomfortable and even angry during class discussions. Below are a few suggestions to help students gather their thoughts and express themselves clearly during a class discussion:

1. Students should be as specific and clear as possible about what they are attempting to express. Being vague in speaking might lead to misinterpretation.

2. Students should take ownership of what they are attempting to express in the discussion. It is best to note during the discussion that the information that they are expressing comes from their frame of reference and perceptions.

3. Students should ask for feedback and listen to others' perspective. Ask follow-up questions like, "Am I being clear? Does that make sense?" Listening to feedback and engaging in a discussion can correct any misperceptions either party may have.

The lecture and discussion model of teaching is a common practice in the university setting. If students master how to clearly and appropriately express themselves during classroom discussions and effectively master taking notes during lectures, then they are well on their way to becoming an excellent student and graduating from college.

Appropriate Student Attire in Class for Male Athletes

What student athletes wear to class says a lot about them and how they think of themselves. Students send out messages by their attire and how they carry themselves on campus. Student athletes send out positive or negative messages with their clothing, and others can make judgments about them—and this remains true on a college campus. Does their attire convey a lack of focus? Does their attire convey intelligence? Does their attire convey professionalism? Does their attire convey mediocrity? A student's attire should convey confidence and show that they have high self-esteem, and it can also set them apart from other students in their classes. Students have only one opportunity to make a first impression and few other chances to make a lasting impression.

There are three basic categories of wardrobe. There is business, business casual, and casual. For men business attire consists of single-breasted blue, grey, or black suit (with only two or three buttons). This may appear conservative, but flamboyantly colored suits are not acceptable in the business arena. There is a difference between dressing sharp and dressing business appropriate. Male students should wear ironed white, blue, or pastel-colored shirts with their dark business suit and they should always wear a t-shirt under their dress shirt. This prevents the dress shirt from becoming stained in the armpit area of the shirt. In business attire, male students should wear ties with small prints or striped design and the tie should stop at the top of one's belt. Belts and shoes should match, and shoes should be polished and well maintained. Bow ties are acceptable, especially on a university campus. Business casual for men usually consists of a dress shirt, pants, and a blazer. It is important that clothes fit properly. Some students have a tendencies to want their pants to sag. When wearing business attire or business casual attire, pants should not sag. Sagging mimics prison culture. Sagging pants developed when prisoners were not allowed to wear belts for fear that belts could be used to hang themselves. The prison policy and the lack of properly sized and ill-fitting prison uniforms brought about the phenomena of sagging, which became popular in hip-hop culture. Male students should wear their pants at their natural waist or just below their belly button and their underwear should not show above their pants. For casual wear it is appropriate for students to wear khakis, jeans, or other pants with golf shirts, button-down shirts, and even T-shirts. Any T-shirt worn should not have profanity or inappropriate messaging on it. Even if it is meant to be humorous, student athletes should remember it could be misinterpreted and send the wrong message to the larger campus community. It is better for student athletes to overdress rather than underdress. If a student goes to see a professor during their office hours, students should wear presentable clothing. Notice that in discussing appropriate attire, expensive versus inexpensive clothing was not discussed. It is of little importance how much a student's clothing costs. It is more important that students wear appropriate, proper fitting, and clean clothes to class rather than attempting to buy expensive clothing.

Appropriate Student Attire in Class for Female Athletes

Female student athletes also convey various messages by the way they dress and carry themselves on campus. As with male attire, there are three basic categories of wardrobe. There is business, business casual, and casual. There should be appropriate distinctions made between the appropriate attire for class, work, church, business and formal affairs, relaxation, and play. Female students should refrain from wearing sheer garments unless they wear proper undergarments to obscure their transparency. Females should also refrain from micro-mini skirts or shorts. Females should wear clothing that covers enough of their thighs while they are standing or sitting. Like with males, females should refrain from wearing T-shirts with profanity or questionable messages on them. Females should not wear ripped jeans or torn jeans to class. They also should not wear bedroom slippers, pajamas, and hair rollers to class.

Female students' business attire should consist of navy blue, black, or gray pencil skirt or pants. Their blouse must be appropriate in style and color (solid) or a solid dress and jacket should be worn. In business attire, females should wear polished shoes with heels two inches or less and closed toes. Female students should limit themselves to three pieces of jewelry (watch, ring, necklace). If female students wear bracelets with their business wear, they should not jingle. Female students' nails should be neatly trimmed and polished in natural tone or clear polish and make sure they have appropriate tone lipstick and makeup. Females should carry a small handbag and wear neutral or dark hosiery.

Students should attempt to wear attire that is appropriate for the climate where their university is located. All students should make sure clothes fit properly by getting pants hemmed and jacket sleeves tailored. Students have only one opportunity to make a first impression and few other chances to make a lasting impression. Some majors will require uniforms such as scrubs for nursing or dental majors, or police uniforms. Nontraditional students who leave work and come directly to class or leave class and go to work may come to class in their uniforms. Students send a message with their attire. Student athletes should start dressing for success and the job that they want while in college.

College Class Schedules

High school course schedules are not like those in college. In high school, students keep the same schedule. Classes are the same Monday through Friday. In college, each class has its own schedule. A student's schedule may be different on each day, and a lot of students opt for a Monday–Wednesday–Friday schedule or a Tuesday–Thursday schedule. In high school, most courses are usually offered between 8:00 a.m. and 3:00 p.m. In college, some classes may be offered during the evenings, weekends, and over the Internet. Students have the choice of when they take their classes. In consultation with an academic advisor or a faculty member, students also have the choice of choosing the particular classes in which they would like to enroll. Most universities have degree plans, which are semester-by-semester course planning sheets to show a student which classes are needed to complete their degree and by which particular time period. Of course, the completion date and graduation depends on the student's ability to pass courses without having to repeat them. Ultimately, it is the students' responsibility to take the courses needed to graduate.

A typical first semester schedule consists of a total course load of 12 to 15 credit hours. At most universities 12 credit hours is considered full-time status. Fifteen hours is suggested during the first semester because a student may have a difficult time adjusting to college life, and this will allow them to drop a course and remain a full-time student. This is important because if a student is receiving federal financial aid they must be a full-time student to receive this benefit. Students are encouraged to see an academic advisor early and often and ask a lot of questions. Advisors are there to help students succeed and adjust to college. There are three primary resources that students should use to determine what courses to take and if they are taking the right courses needed for their major's degree requirement. Their academic advisor or faculty advisor is a great resource in making the correct course choices. Students should always keep a copy of their university's undergraduate catalog. The catalog will specifically lay out which courses are needed to complete a degree for every major offered at the university. Students should also obtain a degree completion plan, which also lays out courses that are needed to complete a degree in a given major. Students should meet with their academic advisor at least once or twice a semester to ensure that they are on track and enrolling in the correct courses for their major. Academic advisors usually do not keep a record of their grades nor can any university official release any information to anyone, including parents if students have not authorized them to do so. The Family Educational Rights and Privacy Act of 1974 prohibits releasing information about students. Therefore, advisors and university administrators will only release general information about policy and procedures.

Time Management and Procrastination

Time management is one of the most important aspects of becoming a successful college student as well as in life. If students do not master time management, they may feel frustration and even anger because they did not complete tasks that they wanted to accomplish. Student athletes must identify and discover techniques to help them manage their time efficiently. In developing good time management techniques, students learn to identify goals they wish to accomplish and then prioritize study activities and assignments. Some students make daily lists of activities, tasks, and assignment due dates. This information can be kept in an electronic planner on a computer or smart phone. If students are "old school," they can write these things down on a note pad, three-by-five cards, or day-planner. It is the student's responsibility to organize their list and keep track of the things that need to be done. Students' lives are not controlled and dictated by outside events. Student athletes can control many aspects of their lives, and students control their lives by the choices that they make. Students must anticipate future external events and control those things that they can control and focus on those things that they can control. Student athletes' lives are not controlled by outside events. Things happen but students must be strong enough to move past these events. If students understand that they control their circumstances and their circumstances do not control them, it will be easier for them to prioritize and develop a plan, and determine in what timeframe their goal must be accomplished despite outside circumstances.

Student athletes should also understand that they cannot meet everyone's expectations. Attempting to fulfill everyone's expectations creates unnecessary pressure on a college student. Unreasonable demands and the expectations of others may be inappropriate for their lifestyle as a college student. By trying to meet the expectations of others, they may be shortchanging themselves and their needs. Student athletes must determine their needs and consider what others expect of them, especially if their goals and priorities are different than the student's. Student athletes should also realize that they are not perfect and that perfectionists are usually very frustrated people. This does not mean that there should not be standards in academics and in living life. It is good to have standards and high expectations, but it is important to avoid becoming a perfectionist. Also, perfectionists are especially prone to procrastination because the perfection they demand is impossible. This may also cause anxiety because perfectionistic goals are impossible to reach.

Procrastination is a key culprit in preventing some student athletes from being successful and graduating from college. There are many types and causes of procrastination. It can take many forms. Student athletes should not allow procrastination to rob them of an opportunity to receive a college degree. There are many reasons why some students procrastinate while in college and do not complete the tasks needed to obtain a degree. Some students simply may not be genuinely interested in obtaining a college degree. If that is the case, they should go and pursue their passion, whatever that may be. Some students find it difficult to begin tasks no matter how simple they may be. Other students are fearful of having their assignments graded, which creates anxiety. Some student athletes may have fallen to peer pressure from those who did not attend college and overvalue what these people think of them. Being a college student has a great deal of uncertainty associated with it, and some students find it difficult to deal with this uncertainty. Last, some students procrastinate because they have low skill sets and procrastination allows them to have an excuse for failing a particular course or assignment. Student athletes must acknowledge their procrastination and identify what has caused them to procrastinate. Poor time management, anxiety, guilt, or low self-esteem may be the cause of procrastination. Students must determine what caused their procrastination and then employ effective strategies to combat it. The following are just a few behaviors associated with procrastination:

- Students ignore tasks, assignments, exams, or term papers, believing by ignoring they will just go away.
- Students underestimate how long it will take to complete a task or overestimate their abilities to complete the task.
- Students believe that mediocrity and poor grades are okay as long as they pass the course with a "C" or "D" grade.
- Students substitute activities that are not associated with the task of studying when it is study time, e.g., clean up the bathrooms as a substitute for studying.
- Students hate making decisions especially when it is left up to them, e.g., choosing a paper topic or partners for a group project.

Effective planning is an excellent tool in combating procrastination. Student athletes should make long-term and short-term plans but avoid overplanning. Students must take ownership and make sincere decisions about their work and how they work. Students who choose to spend a minimal amount of time on their school work have no one else to blame but themselves and should admit this if results are not up to standard. If students only want to devote small amounts of time to a task like studying and reading textbooks, that is their choice, but they must be willing to deal with the consequence of this action.

There are strategies that students can employ to prevent procrastination. Students can break down a larger task into smaller tasks. Students should also determine a reasonable timeframe to complete assignments and studying. Often, students underestimate the time required for an assignment or believe they can do more than is humanly possible. Students should also realize that relaxation is needed, especially after long periods of work. There is time for relaxation while accomplishing tasks associated with school. It is a good practice for students to monitor their progress on the small tasks and when problems occur, address them early to avoid these problems becoming bigger problems in the future. Student athletes must be reasonable about the expectations of themselves, their abilities, and the college experience. Most of all they should not sabotage themselves when they are making progress toward obtaining a degree. Student athletes should remember that they are college students and the responsibility is solely theirs to graduate. College is not like high school; there is no more just sitting in structured days where one can get away with only marginally studying. In college there may be days where students have three to six classes with heavy reading loads and assignments for each class. A college student must negotiate their time between many competing interests. Students must realize that procrastination will help end their time on a university campus very quickly, and they should never be afraid to ask for help.

STEP TWELVE: GRADUATING, GOING PRO, OR FINDING OTHER GAINFUL EMPLOYMENT

Career Choices

For a collegiate student athlete, finding a job after college is no different than for the general student population. Collegiate athletics may consume some athletes. However, when the athlete's eligibility is exhausted, there are choices that former student athletes must make. Each former college athlete should determine what he or she wishes to do after his or her collegiate athletic career is over. This requires student athletes to have thought about possible careers and developed plans to reach their career goals. Student athletes should use their university's career services office. In most cases, the personnel in career services will assist with a job search or connect students with alumni who are in the field of their choice. Career service offices also help students with constructing résumés, cover letters, and mock job interviews. Résumés should not be generic. They should cater to the specific jobs that students are seeking. Résumés should highlight and showcase their skills and achievements.

Student athletes should spend time networking. They should join professional development clubs or an industry group. Clubs and groups can connect students with established professionals in specific areas of interest. This also allows student athletes to connect with possible mentors that can help guide them in the future. Student athletes should also create a LinkedIn profile. This will allow them to build a network and possibly gain work experience. As they gain more experience, they can delete early jobs and add better ones. If possible, student athletes should participate in internships in a career field of interest. There are many places to network. Below are just a few to consider:

- Career fairs
- College alumni associations
- Professional organizations
- Conferences
- Job shadowing opportunities
- Internship or volunteering

Also finding a good job coach may be helpful. A good job coach can assist student athletes in avoiding costly mistakes and avoid many frustrations by helping with the following:

- Put together a list of potential employers
- Identify those with contacts potential employers

- Research potential employers
- Have student athlete's contacts review their résumé
- Watch student athlete's social footprint

Campus Career Center

As a collegiate athlete's career comes to a close, they should begin to think about their career options. College campuses have career centers that assist students with finding employment after college. Career centers offer students programs, services, professional development, and other resources to help them find employment in various fields. Career centers aim to help students thrive professionally in their chosen fields of endeavor. Career centers help students develop skills, market their skills, assess themselves and their abilities, and explore career options. The career center can help student athletes discover their major of choice and also discover various interests. It may also help students build or refine résumés and work on interviewing. With interviewing services, student athletes can practice over-the-phone interviews, Skype interviews, or face-to-face interviews. These activities include crafting great personal statements and cover letters. Career centers also offer various workshops and networking events to help students meet potential employers. The career center's literature and videos can assist student athletes in career exploration. Most career centers offer mock interview programs where students can refine their interviewing skills. Career centers also offer a way to explore potential career choices by shadowing someone who works in that career. For instance, if a student athlete wants to become a dentist, an excellent option to find out more about this career would be to follow a dentist to find out what her typical workday involves. Student athletes may also choose to interview a professional in their field of interest. If an interview is granted, student athletes should take notes. Below are a few questions that could be asked:

What is your typical workday like?

What do you like most (and least) about your job?

What skills/abilities are most important to succeed in this job?

What is your educational background?

How did you get started in this field?

What courses were most helpful to you and which would you recommend?

What is the best way to get started in this field?

Do you have any additional advice to help me prepare?

Even if a student athlete is going into professional sports, the career center may help them brush up on their interview skills.

Graduate School

Some student athletes will choose to attend graduate or professional school after they graduate and their collegiate athletic career is over. To pursue a graduate degree a student must have received an undergraduate degree. Graduate school constitutes an advanced program of study that is focused on a particular academic discipline. Traditionally, graduate school centers on producing research in a discipline and developing knowledge of a particular profession. Graduate study is more of a concentrated course of study, and the expectations of graduate and undergraduate study are different. Graduate school has a higher expectation in regards to quality of work, and there is more work assigned in graduate school compared to undergraduate school. Graduate study is concentrated within a specific discipline, and there are not as many elective courses to choose from. Graduate classes have fewer students than an undergraduate class with much more student discussion and interaction. The grading in graduate study is more rigorous than undergraduate study, and student work may be evaluated by peers. After a student athlete's career, they may wish to pursue a graduate degree, be it a specialist degree, master's degree, or doctoral degree. A specialist degree in addition to a master's degree. This degree usually prepares a student for particular certifications in a given field. A master's degree usually is designed to lead to a doctoral degree; however, this may not always be the case. A master's degree program is usually a two-year course of study. The doctoral degree is the highest degree possible. It usually requires creating new knowledge through independent research. It usually takes five to seven years to complete the course work and defend a dissertation.

Sports Agents

Sports agents are individuals who help athletes manage their careers. A sports agent may work with one player or multiple players from various professional sports leagues. Sports agents are there to seek answers and help athletes with concerns or requests. Sports agents should be trustworthy and have a great relationship with the athletes whom they represent. It is important to remember that an agent works for the athlete, not the inverse. This relationship must be built on trust and groomed. Sports agents should be experts at networking and should assist the athletes they work with to improve their networks. They should be aware of trends and the latest happenings in the world of sports. This allows the agent to provide the best advice to their athletes and keep them abreast of developments on the business side of professional sports. Sports agents also help athletes build a good reputation. They are great at risk management. In building this good reputation, they ensure that the athlete will be in high demand for possible endorsement deals. Most often, sports agents handle accounting and legal duties associated with the professional athlete. The agent markets the athlete to professional teams in respective sports to secure employment or a more lucrative contract for an athlete. A sports agent handles the delicate details of the contract such as the length of the contract, benefits, salary, and other stipulations of the athlete. Agents negotiate contracts and provide advice about business deals. Agents may also set up product endorsement deals. Shoe, clothing, and other entities have turned to athletes and their agents to help increase the brand and sales of their products.

In some cases, an agent helps the athlete manage their finances. In doing so, the agent should keep meticulous records of wages, sponsorship benefits, and small market investments. It is important to note that collegiate athletes are not allowed to sign with an agent or even to have contact with an agent until they have declared themselves for a professional sport's draft or they have exhausted their college athletic eligibility.

Professional Sports

With the massive popularity of professional sports, there are young people who dream of becoming a professional athlete. Statistically of the 100,000 high school seniors who participate in football each year, only a few of them will ever make it to the NFL. Only about 9,000 players go on to play football on the college level; only a few are invited to the NFL Scouting Combine. Only 53 players are on each of the 32 teams in the NFL. That means there are only approximately 1,700 players in the NFL each season. The average football player's career is only about three years. In the NFL, there are no guaranteed contracts, and an athlete may find himself quickly unemployed if football is all he concentrated on in college. There are multimillion-dollar contracts in the NFL, but the minimum salary for a rookie is $325,000. There is a sliding scale that is used with the additional years of experience gained, so a second-year player can average $395,000 and a third-year player can earn $470,000. These salaries are great on the surface, but remember the average football career is just three years, so it is imperative to not put all of one's efforts on becoming a professional athlete. A first-year player's salary is composed of three things: base salary, prorated signing bonus, and future bonuses. Other incentives written into a player's contract do not go toward a team's rookie salary pool figure. NFL teams play 16 regular season games over a 17-week period. Games are played on Monday, Thursday, Sunday, and some Saturdays. Most games kick off at 1:00, 4:05, 4:25, or 8:30 p.m.

Unlike the National Football League, the National Basketball Association (NBA) and Major League Baseball (MLB) offer players guaranteed contracts for the length of the contract's entirety from the moment that the contract is executed and signed. The NBA consists of 30 teams. Twenty-nine of these teams are in the United States and there is one NBA team in Canada. Teams play an 82-game season from October through April with playoff games beginning in April and the championship in June. The initial term of an NBA rookie contract is just two years. NBA teams may exercise an option to re-sign a rookie for a third season, if they wish. This option may be exercised after the completion of the player's initial season. First-round rookie contracts increase each year, but the player's salary depends on when he was drafted. For instance, the number-one draft pick will earn more than the number-two pick. In 2014–2015, the NBA's rookie top draft pick made just under $5 million. NBA players are paid biweekly. The standard paydays are the 1st and 15th of each month, beginning on November 15. Players can have their pay distributed over 12 months and receive 12 or 36 months depending on their preference. Advances, signing bonuses, loans, and deferred compensation may be paid on nonscheduled pay dates. At the opening of the 2015–2016, there were only 446 players in the NBA.

In Major League Baseball (MLB), there are 30 teams with approximately 40 players on each roster per major league team. This means that only 848 players can play major league baseball in a given season. Baseball season usually opens during the first week of April and lasts through September or October. Contracts in baseball are guaranteed. According to Eric Stephen of SB Nation, the intent of the collective bargaining agreement between Major League Baseball and the Players Association, during the years from 2012–2016, stipulated minimum salaries of $480,000 in 2012, $490,000 in 2013, and $500,000 in 2014. This defined the minimum salary for the 2015 season at $507,500. Stephen also states "players on a major league active roster also receive a daily meal and tip allowance for every date a team is on the road plus any travel day. That daily amount will increase from $99.00 to $100.50 in 2015." There are 162 games played during a season of major league baseball.

The Women's National Basketball Association (WNBA) has 12 teams. Teams play a 34-game season. The season usually begins in May and concludes in September. The league requires draft entrants to be at least 22 years old during the year in which the draft takes place and have no remaining college eligibility or renounce any future college eligibility. In 2014, the average salary of WNBA players was $72,000 per year. The WNBA's minimum league salary was $37,950. The league's top salary was $107,000 for players who had been in the league for six years or more. On average, WNBA teams pay a total of approximately $10.4 million to 144 players. In comparing salaries of the male and female professional basketball leagues, there were 52 NBA players who made more than the entire WNBA combined. The WNBA league maximum has been slowly increasing; their salaries still do not compare to the salaries of players in the NBA. WNBA players made a maximum of $101,000 per year, yet the average salary for NBA players was $5 million. Due to these inequities and wage disparities, many WNBA players have chosen to play in international leagues in other countries where they can make better salaries. As of 2014, the highest-paid player in the WNBA was Candace Parker. Parker subsidized her salary with endorsement deals with various companies. She has accumulated an estimated net worth of roughly $3 million. Players have called for the maximum salary to increase to only $121,500 by 2021.

Major League Soccer (MLS) is composed of 20 teams. There are 17 teams in the United States and three teams in Canada. The MLS regular season goes from March to October. Each team plays 34 games. In 2016, the average major league soccer player made $141,903.13. The salary cap is $3.1 million per team, not counting the extra salary of designated players. Teams are not independently owned. Each team is owned and controlled by investors in the league. In the National Women's Soccer League, as of 2013 players' salaries ranged from $6,842 to $30,000.

The National Hockey League consists of 30 teams. There are 23 teams in the United States and seven teams in Canada. The regular season consists of 82 games lasting from October through April. Players younger than 25 years of age during the year of their first NHL contract must sign an entry-level contract. Entry-level contracts have restrictions and allowable salary amounts for young players. The maximum allowable salary for a player's entry-level contract is $925,000. The length of the entry-level contract is also dependent on the player's age. Players who are 18–21 years of age must sign a three-year contract. Players who are 22–23 years of age must sign a two-year contract, and players who are 24 years of age must sign a one-year contract. According to Cap Friendly, signing and performance bonuses can be included in entry-level contracts. Signing bonuses may not exceed more than 10 percent of the contract's total compensation, to be paid to players annually. There are two types of performance bonuses, one of which includes league awards and trophies, as well as bonuses agreed upon by a player and the club that signed him, which cannot exceed $2 million per season. Any bonuses attached to league awards or trophies are paid by the league and are not captured within the actual entry-level contract signed by the player.

Professional sports may seem a quick ticket to success. However, as this section shows, if a student athlete does go pro, a career in sports can be short-lived. In most cases, college student athletes overestimate their chances of going professional in sports. Some universities that have had student athletes who transition to become professionals in sports feed student athletes these dreams from the time they are being recruited. Although with some athletes, this seed is being planted in their heads during their first recruiting call and the odds are they will not become a professional in sports, schools use this as an edge when recruiting against opposing schools. Universities continue to use successful professional athletes from their schools as trophies hoping that high school athletes will choose their school to further their dreams of playing professional sports. This can also be exploitative for student athletes from low-income communities looking for an escape from poverty. All collegiate athletes should remember college athletics should be primarily a means to obtaining a college degree.

SUGGESTED READING

Bimper, Albert Y., Jr. "Game Changers: The Role Athletic Identity and Racial Identity Play on Academic Performance." *Journal of College Student Development* 55, no. 8 (2014): 795–807.
Carter, Akilah R., and Algerian Hart. "Perspectives of Mentoring: The Black Female Student-Athlete." *Sports Management Review* 13, no. 4 (2010): 382–394.

Carter-Francique, Akilah R., Algerian Hart, and Geremy Cheeks. "Examining the Value of Social Capital and Social Support for Black Student-Athlete's Academic Success." *Journal of African American Studies* 19, no. 2 (2015): 157–177.

Covey, Stephen R. *The 7 Habits of Highly Effective People: Restoring the Character Ethic.* New York: Simon & Schuster, 1989.

Edwards, J., and Jennifer Hargreaves. "Sport Feminism." In *International Encyclopedia of Women and Sports*, edited by Karen Christensen, Allen Guttmann, and Gertrud Pfister, 395–402. New York: Macmillan, 2001.

Fertman, Carl I. *Student-Athlete Success: Meeting the Challenges of College Life.* Sudbury, MA: Jones and Bartlett Publishers, 2008.

Gladwell, Malcolm. *Outliers: The Story of Success.* New York: Little, Brown and Company, 2010.

Harrison, C. Keith. "Perceptions of African American Male Student-Athletes in Higher Education." Unpublished dissertation, School of Education, University of Southern California, 1995.

National Collegiate Athletic Association. "Cost of Attendance Q&A." Last modified September 3, 2015. http://www.ncaa.com/news/ncaa/article/2015–09–03/cost-attendance-qa

Sailes, Gary. "An Investigation of Campus Stereotypes: The Myth of Black Athletic Superiority and the Dumb Jock Stereotype." *Sociology of Sport Journal* 10, no. 1 (1993): 88–97.

PART VI

Student Athletes' Experiences and After the Cheering Stops

In this section, former student athletes discuss their undergraduate experiences. They provide advice to those seeking to compete in college athletics. The participants' demographic backgrounds are varied. Participants are both male and female. They are from urban and rural environments. Some of these former student athletes received scholarships while others did not. They participated in various sports, had varied majors, and were involved in various extracurricular activities. Some of these student athletes transferred schools during their career while others competed at the same school for all four years of their eligibility. Each participant was asked to respond to several questions about their undergraduate studies and their experience as student athletes. There are a few common themes that emerged from the participants' responses.

It is apparent that most of the student athletes who received scholarships were appreciative of this financial award because it alleviated concerns about how they would pay for their college education. Some student athletes used a combination of scholarships and loans to pay for their education. However, all of the former student athletes stated that having a good support system of family, friends, coaches, and athletic support personnel was essential to their success. Most of them talked about developing strong relationships with their teammates and how these bonds continued after they were no longer student athletes. With all of the competing demands, the former student athletes believe that time management was the most important skill to master as a student athlete. Most of them found the adjustment from high school to college difficult in athletics and academics, but appreciated the structured and regimented schedule that student athletes followed. They also realized that they lived in a "fish bowl": they believe they were held to a higher standard than the general student population.

Many of the student athletes believed they were stereotyped because they were athletes. Some people believe that athletes were less intelligent or had it easier because they were college athletes. Most of the students prided themselves in being student athletes and credit this experience in their undergraduate success. They also credit participating in college athletics with teaching them how to overcome adversity and sharpen their leadership skills. The participants also believe that being student athletes helped them become better people. The majority of the participants were extremely appreciative of the opportunities that being a student athlete brought them. They also acknowledged that their time as a college student athlete passed quickly; therefore they urged future student athletes to treasure their time and urged them to find good peers and mentors and to surround themselves with people who truly care about them and want to see them to succeed.

Note: At the request of the interviewees, some of the last names have been removed or respondents have opted for anonymity.

ATHLETE 1

Name: Jessie Lantz

Sport(s) Played: Volleyball

University Attended: Western Illinois University

Years Attended: 6

Undergraduate Degree: Bachelor of Arts in Communication and Bachelor of Science in Recreation Administration

Highest Degree Obtained: Master of Science in Sport Management

Parent(s) Occupation: High school teacher and laboratory technician

Current Occupation: Graduate assistant

Ethnicity: White

Gender: Female

I chose my undergraduate institution because I wanted to play Division I volleyball. I was already very interested in the academic programs available. The university's location was in close proximity to my home town. This made it an easy choice because it was convenient and manageable. Coming out of high school, I did not receive a scholarship. However, I did not receive a scholarship until my sophomore season. During my freshman year, I was a walk-on with a guarantee that I would get one the following year. This helped me in making my final decision to attend the university. The possibility of receiving a scholarship motivated me to attend college. I had siblings who were also attending college; therefore it was essential that I should find some financial assistance to fund my higher education.

Academically, my transition from high school to college was fairly easy because I managed my time well, prior to attending college. I was committed to my academic program. I knew attending college was the best choice for me. I could be successful because I manage my time well. Those students who cannot master time management will have difficulty in succeeding in college, especially attempting to balance athletics and academics. After I discovered that this was the best place for me academically, I did not think about transferring to another school. Athletically, it took some time for me to become confident in my athletic abilities. I assumed I would not be called on as a leader especially during my freshman year. I discovered each member of the team was a leader in their own right. Each member has to exhibit leadership as soon as the team had formed.

I used scholarships and student loans to ease the financial burden of tuition and fees. This allowed me to concentrate on academics and athletics without having the burden of worrying about how I would pay for my college education. I found that there were so many resources available for student athletes at my university. As an athlete, we received academic resources such as free tutoring and academic advising. I found there to be numerous resources and people to support me in achieving my goals as a student and an athlete. To be successful as a college athlete, I made sure to take advantage of study hall hours when they were scheduled. I also refined my time management skills. I started using my electronic devices like the calendar on my phone to keep track of where I had to be and when.

Having strong relationships is a key to succeeding in college. I believe it is important to maintain close relationships when in undergraduate school; especially when you are involved in athletics. It has always been important to me to remain close with my family. I turn to them for insight and support on many occasions, especially when I am experiencing difficulties academically, athletically, or socially. Additionally, having strong and close relationships with teammates will help you continue success. As an athlete, you do spend an enormous of time around teammates, so it is best to develop some relationships and make some friends on the team.

Therefore, two things helped me be successful in college. In college athletics, I found that I had to be mentally tough. Being mentally tough was so important as a student athlete because you could not dwell on disappointments or mistakes. You have to have a short memory and be ready for the next play. You must quickly assess and evaluate situations, then adjust and move on. Mental toughness can be helpful whether it is in academics or athletics. My faith also played a part in my success. I grew up in the Methodist denomination. I went to church just about every Sunday and in college, I continued this as my time allowed. I have been consistent in my faith and this has helped me. I did not join a Greek-lettered organization while I was an undergraduate. I did become a member of the Student Recreation Society (SRS). My membership in this organization allowed me to develop relationships with other people in my major and also learn how all of my courses served a purpose and how each course was relevant to the overall curriculum.

I was so fortunate to be a collegiate athlete. I often suggest to young athletes that when you find it difficult to balance academics and athletics, it is stressful, and the pressure begins to build, remember how fortunate you are to be able to continue playing the sport you love. It is the love of the sport that will see you through. Participating in sports helped contribute to my success as an undergraduate student. It seems I have always succeeded when I had tons of things to do. By staying extremely busy, it kept me focused on the task at hand and allowed me to manage my time and successfully graduate as a student athlete.

ATHLETE 2

Name: Jil Price

Sport(s) Played: Softball collegiately, cross country in high school

University Attended: Indiana University–Purdue University, Fort Wayne (IPFW)

Undergraduate Degree: Bachelor of Arts in Communications with minors in Journalism and Media and Public Relations

Highest Degree Obtained: Master of Science in Kinesiology and Sport Management

Parent(s) Occupation: Father, real estate agent; mother, front office secretary at an elementary school

Current Occupation: Assistant Director of Athletic Communications at the University of Iowa

Ethnicity: Caucasian

Gender: Female

Initially, I was set to attend Indiana University and join the softball team as a preferred walk-on. It was late in the recruiting process and I thought I would be a walk on at Indiana University. Late in the recruiting process, I received a scholarship offer from Indiana–Purdue Fort Wayne (IPFW) to play softball. After receiving the scholarship offer, I accepted the scholarship offer. If I had not received an athletic scholarship offer, I probably would not have attended IPFW. I always knew I wanted to attend college. There was no doubt in my mind that I would not accomplish this goal. I knew that I needed to obtain a scholarship. By receiving an athletic scholarship, I knew that it would benefit financially, socially, and professionally.

When I accepted the athletic scholarship offer at IPFW, I had a backup plan. I knew I would attend Indiana University if things did not work out at IPFW. I wanted to pursue a career in journalism or communication. This major was attractive because if I transferred to Indiana University, I would have only two academic years to complete my degree. I ultimately decided to diversify my major to enhance my educational experiences as an undergraduate. Ultimately, I chose communications as a major with minors in journalism, media, and publications. I believe that my undergraduate experience was well-rounded. This major prepared me for a multitude of jobs in print as well as other media related jobs.

Transitioning from high school to college was very difficult for me. During my first year, it was difficult to balance student life and athletics. I had to chart the best way to balance my life as a student, athlete, and socialite. I had to learn all of those things on my own. Eventually, I figured it out and I was able to move forward and be a good student and collegiate athlete. I am a first-generation college student. My parents did not complete college. My mother attended college for one semester and dropped out. My father began a career in to real estate shortly after he graduated from high school. My parents have a blue collar work ethic and they have worked very hard to become successful. They have transferred the belief that "you can accomplish anything through hard work" and that is the motto that I live by.

Since my parents did not go to college, they believe that it was necessary to assist me and my siblings in any way possible so that we could complete college. My parents gave each of us $2,000 per year toward our college education during our undergraduate studies. This money combined with my softball scholarship helped ease the financial burden of paying for college. I also worked two jobs every summer and one job during softball off-season to pay for the rest of my college education.

I found the educational resources on my campus to be plentiful, especially for college athletes. We had academic advisors who worked with us to guide us in selecting the proper courses and to keep us on the right academic path. We also had tutors available to assist us with our studies. They worked around our classes and practice schedules to ensure that we were prepared for our exams and class assignments. When I needed help or assistance, someone was always there to help me.

My most important relationships in college were with my coaches, administrators, and support staff. These individuals recognized leadership traits in me before I recognized these traits in myself. I am very appreciative that they helped develop my leadership skills. I continue to have several mentors from my undergraduate years. They have continued to advise me and give me guidance. My most memorable relationships while as an undergraduate was with my teammates. I still keep in contact with several of them even though some of them live in other states and outside the United States. I count them as true friends and, no matter what phase of life we are in, I plan to continue these friendships. I am truly thankful to have those friendships develop during my time as a college athlete and continue long term.

In regards to my racial and gender identity, I believe that I was judged by my outer appearance. Some of my classmates called me a "little rich white girl." This was far from the truth. As an exercise in one of my communication courses, the professor had individuals in the class to size up and stereotype classmates. This was followed by individuals revealing their truths. Many of my classmates thought that I came from a wealthy background with an easy life. They also speculated I probably had a nice car and very materialistic and life was easy for me. When I revealed the truth, many of my classmates were shocked that I was far from the stereotype they had constructed.

As an athlete, learning to handle any disappointments or failures can be difficult. During my first year, I suffered a season-ending injury. While injured, I learned how to handle failure. I gained a different perspective on life and my sport during my time out, which helped me return to the field in a more mature manner. I have always known that I would have to overcome adversity. It was easier after I recovered from this injury because I had the opportunity gain a new perspective when I was away from the game. I think having the game taken away from me gave me the opportunity to respect the game much more. This injury also taught me how to fulfill my role in any situation.

I used three things to get me through my undergraduate studies; study tables, study groups, and caffeine! We were required to spend four hours of undistracted time in study tables each week as softball student athletes. Studying in this structured environment was very good for me, but it was annoying sometimes because I would complete my assignments quickly and then have to find something to do for the rest of the allotted time. When I studied on my own, I never finished as quickly. I also used a planner, which contained my softball schedule, academic, work, and social commitments. I know that a planner seems kind of old school now, but this was prior to having team apps on smart phone devices which so many student athletes use now.

When I look back on my time as a student athlete, it's all about establishing and maintaining balancing in your life. I found myself focusing on one aspect or another too much in my first year, which taught me some hard lessons at times. I did find time to work in extracurricular activities; I was a member of the student athlete athletic leadership team (SALT) at IPFW. I was also the copy editor for the IPFW student newspaper. I was selected as the homecoming queen during my sophomore year. This honor allowed me to be a standing member on homecoming committee. I found a church near IPFW that I really made a connection with. I was able to attend on Sunday services and I eventually stared leading a youth group for middle school young teens on Wednesdays. When I was in season and traveling on Sundays, I would watch a video stream or listen to audio of the sermon each week. My grandfather is a minister, so I grew up knowing the Lord and wanted to continue to have that aspect of my life in college. By being involved in campus activities, it allowed me to develop my leadership skills.

Any successful college student athlete must have maturity, confidence, organization, and a good work ethic. I believe these elements are the keys to the success of a college student athlete. Many of the skills that you learn on the field are transferrable skills. If they are determined and have the drive in and out of the athletic arena, they will be successful in life. Participating in sports helped give me a sense of pride and it gave me a platform. I was proud to stand out as a student athlete. I also enjoyed the pressure it put on me to be a success in every area. Be it be academically, athletically, or even now in the professional sphere. Through sports, I learned to appreciate the journey and go through the process of being a student athlete. Regardless of your role on the team, being a college athlete is one of the best experiences that a person can have. It has prepared me for so many things. Collegiate athletics helped me become to be strong mentally and physically and sharpen my leadership skills.

ATHLETE 3

Name: Chris

Sport(s) Played: Basketball

University Attended: Central Michigan University

Years Attended: 2009–2013 (medical redshirt senior year)

Undergraduate Degree: Sports Management

Highest Degree Obtained: Master of Science

Parent(s) Occupation: Father, high school teacher; mother, commercial property manager

Current Occupation: Marketing representative

Ethnicity: White

Gender: Male

I chose my undergraduate institution because I was offered a scholarship. I had always dreamed of playing Division I college basketball. Central Michigan University helped me fulfill that dream. I am very thankful that they gave me this opportunity. I accepted the scholarship part because I liked the coaching staff and players I met while on my official recruiting visit. We immediately developed a bond. I trusted them to help me both on the court and off the court.

My transition from high school to college was difficult because I was away from home. I was in a new state and nine hours away from the familiarity and comfort of home. I was away from my family and friends. Even though I had my teammates, I still wondered if I would fit in and easily make new friends when I was not around the team.

The biggest difference was the freedom you inherit. You are free to make all kinds of choices. When I was growing up, I always relied on my parents to help me make decisions. Moving away to college helped me grow as an adult. It also made me more independent and it forced me to make my own decisions. Moreover, I learned that I could not blame anyone for my decisions and I had to live with the consequences of those decisions. As I reflect on my decision to go to college away from my home town, I am glad I went away to as far as I did. Going away to college forced me to become more outgoing, which is an essential quality in the sales occupation I currently work in.

I was pretty confident in my basketball skills because I had great coaching growing up. I also knew there were a few areas that needed improving in my game. I was a little nervous entering my freshman year because the players were bigger and stronger than me. I had a great support network of people who would encourage me and my game started to improve. It took a few games to get used to the pace, the physicality, and the atmosphere, but I knew I belonged at that level. As the season advanced, my game and my confidence advanced.

The fact that I had a scholarship freed me from worrying about how I was going to pay for college. It was very reassuring that my entire college education was going to be paid for. I never worried about money while in college. I realize that I was very lucky. My parents had steady careers and I knew I had their support if I needed it. Young student athletes should remember hard work eventually gets rewarded. Maybe, the rewards will not come right away but I believe there are a few things that will help you become a success. If you have a strong faith in God, a good work ethic, and good teammates, and are a coachable athlete, you will be rewarded. If you truly believe in yourself and your abilities, you will be rewarded one way or another.

I had to deal with a lot of adversity as a student athlete. I had to fight through the tough times and this has made me believe that I can conquer any challenge that life brings to me. This was first instilled in me through my dad. He was also my coach all the way through high school. He taught me to never give up because that is the easiest thing to do. Playing college sports is a huge challenge and there are only a small percentage of athletes who have the opportunity to do it. I am thankful that I was one of those people. It was one of the best experiences of my life and I wouldn't have traded it for anything else.

I think the most important relationships you can acquire as a college athlete are the relationships you have with your coaches and teammates. These are people you go to work with, bleed, sweat, cry, hurt, and accomplish your goals with. Those are the bonds and memories you will never forget. You experience every single emotion with these people and they will make you grow as an athlete and as a person. They sort of become like your family away from home. Having these relationships helps put your foot in the door to numerous opportunities. I have also formed great relationships with many alumni and supporters of our basketball program and these people are excellent resources for networking.

I had difficulties on the court and in the classroom. On the court, I did not have a really good relationship with my head coach during my junior and senior year. Before my sophomore year, we got a new coach and the coach that recruited me left the program. The coaching change may be a factor for why my college career was not as successful as I had hoped it would be. Under the new coach, there were times when I felt like I was being treated unfairly. I believed that I was a victim of racial discrimination. During this difficult time, I leaned on my family and friends for support. I also relied on some of my closest teammates for encouragement and advice on how to get through it. There were days that I felt like quitting, but I remembered the lessons that my dad had taught me. I was raised not to be a quitter.

I leaned on my family and friends and closest teammates for support on the court. My struggles in the classroom were mostly my fault. Most of the time, my difficulties in the classroom occurred because I did not manage my time well. I had to face the fact that it was my responsibility to take academics seriously. I had to take a good look at my time management and extracurricular activities and get back on track academically. Time management is one of the most important skills that need to be mastered as a student athlete. If you can manage your time more than likely you can be successful.

At Central Michigan University all student athletes were required to attend study hall every week. The amount of time that you were required to spend in study hall was based on your grade point average. The higher the grade point average, the less time you needed to spend in study hall and vice versa. To stay focused and on track, I kept a student planner. I wrote in my planner every appointment and every day to make sure my assignments were completed on time.

There are many lessons and words of wisdom that student athletes can use during their college athletic careers. There are five important lessons that I have gained during my collegiate athletic experience: learn to manage your time efficiently, form bonds with your coaches and teammates as well as avid supporters of the athletic program, understand that adversity is part of being a student athlete and if you can learn to overcome it (whether on a small or large scale) it will help you succeed after you graduate, academics should come before athletics, and the most important thing about going to college is obtaining your degree. College sports can have very demanding schedules but it is essential that you make time for your studies; understand that as a representative of an athletic program, you are held to a higher standard than any other student at the school. Student athletes are constantly put under a microscope and people in the community are always going to be watching every move you make. It is your obligation to put on a good face and to be a good representative of your program by staying out of trouble, being courteous to all of the fans and citizens of the community, and making sure your teammates do the same.

I believe playing sports in college helped me grow as a student because I loved playing basketball so much. I knew that if I did not perform in the classroom, I could not compete in athletics. This has served as a huge motivation for me. It was this motivation that helped me stay focused on tasks at hand that I currently face today. If I do not complete my required work today in my current job, I will lose my job and will not make money. Playing Division I college basketball was one of the best experiences of my life and it benefited me immensely. I got to travel the country, and play a game that I loved and have been around since I could walk. It gave me the opportunity to go places I never would have gone and meet people that I would not have met. These experiences helped shape who I am, and I encourage any student athlete to take advantage of the opportunity to play sports in college if given one. There will be tough times along the way but the overall experience and the memories you make in four or five years will last a lifetime.

ATHLETE 4

Name: Dustin Vissering
Sport(s) Played: Baseball
University Attended: Illinois Central College (ICC)

Years Attended: 2006–2008

Undergraduate Degree: Bachelor of Science in Athletic Training

Highest Degree Obtained: Master of Science in Sport Management

Parent(s) Occupation: Father, client services director

Current Occupation: Athletic trainer with the Texas Rangers Baseball Club

Ethnicity: Caucasian

Gender: Male

After graduating from high school, I attended Illinois Central College (ICC). ICC is a community college and I wanted to become an elementary school teacher. I did not receive a scholarship to attend my undergraduate institution. I was still drawn to ICC because it was close to home but far enough away to live on my own as an adult. The academic strength the school had in my field was strong. After taking a few classes, I discovered that becoming an elementary school teacher was not a good occupational fit for me. After I received my associate's degree I transferred to a four-year institution as Illinois State University. I discovered that Illinois State University had an accredited athletic training program, where I eventually earned a degree in that field. The transition from high school to college was difficult for me. The academic workload and expectations were increased heavily. I was not a good student in high school, and I had to learn how to be a good student in college. Obviously, when talking about sports becoming a collegiate athlete versus a high school athlete is as different as night and day.

Collegiate athletics was different than high school because college athletes are bigger, stronger, and faster. In addition, the speed of the game on the college level is greater. I grew up a confident kid so I always believed my talent would translate in college. When things got tough as motivation, I envisioned a better life that my college education would give me. I wanted to better myself and have a better life. I had a small academic scholarship to attend community college but after that I was on my own financially. I took out loans to attend Illinois State University. My dad assisted me after I completed my undergraduate degree. My dad helped me pay off my student loans.

Successful athletes make good choices. This is important for your success in college. Your environment shapes you as a person. If you do not have positive people in your corner whether these people are family members, friends or professors, more than likely you will struggle. I believe that to be successful, you must surround yourself with positive people positive influences. This will play a major role in your success.

I believe my gender played a role as an undergraduate student because of the specific program I was involved in. Athletic training is a field that is traditionally dominated by males. This may be because athletic training allows a person to be inside the locker room and closely involved with the players. In the past, there were not as many female athletic trainers in professional sports as there are now. I believe that being male helped me to land an internship with a minor league baseball team, while I was still in college. I do not believe I would have had the same opportunities if I were a female.

I am a firm believer that if a person has not failed then they have yet to live a full life. I have learned from my failures. College athletics will teach you how to rebound and overcome failure. Sports taught me how to take instruction and make adjustments in moving forward and completing projects. For example, if my boss is unhappy with my work and notifies me about what he does not like about it, I can guarantee you that I will not make the same mistake again. As a student athlete, I relied heavily on library time. This was important to mastering my studies. There were too many distractions at the apartment like, video games, movies, and friends. I was highly successful when I removed myself from that environment and went to the library to complete homework. I also found a close friend in the same field to study with.

I would always bounce questions off each other and challenge ourselves. I have always been a believer in Jesus Christ. I attended church every so often in college. I find that college stands for everything the Bible does not want you to be most times. Even though, I did not attend church as much during college I did hide that I was a follower of Christ if the discussion surfaced. I believe student athletes should be self-discipline but they should not follow the crowd and do the same thing other athletes are doing. Student athletes should spend less time on social media and pick up a book to help you grow as a professional. They should create conversation with people instead of texting all the time.

ATHLETE 5

Name: Emmett Gill

Sport(s) Played: Baseball

University Attended: University of North Carolina Charlotte

Years Attended: 1987–1991

Undergraduate Degree: Psychology

Highest Degree Obtained: Doctorate

Parent(s) Occupation: Librarian/principal

Current Occupation: Assistant professor/national coordinator

Ethnicity: Black

Gender: Male

I chose my undergraduate institution because it was an in-state school and it offered the major that I was interested. It also offered me the best chance to play baseball. Initially, I attended the University of North Carolina, Chapel Hill but I transferred to University of North Carolina, Charlotte. I received a scholarship after I qualified academically. With all of these factors, I believe that UNC Charlotte was the best place for me. I probably did not take college as seriously as

I should have. In describing myself as a young student athlete, I was young, dumb, and trying to have fun, therefore attempting to obtain a scholarship did not motivate me that much.

It was difficult transitioning from high school to college for many reasons. There was lots of freedom. I had to figure out the best way to manage time, money, and energy. I found the coursework was not that challenging from high school to college. I struggled with time management. Having fun was my priority, so I found it difficult to complete my class assignments. I was a trying to fit studying in between having fun. I believe that student athletes should not just choose a major because they believe that it may give them an opportunity to make money. They should pursue their passion and choose to study they are passionate about. This was an important factor in choosing my undergraduate major.

Competing in college athletics helped me become a good student and a successful person. I remember one instance when I almost got kicked off the team because of poor grades. After dealing with this academic setback, I consistently made the honor roll. I was truly blessed that I had a coach and professors who cared about my well-being. Seeing how they cared about my success, this allowed me to get on the right track and motivated me to begin caring about my own success.

My athletic, academic and social experiences were balanced. I believe that the most important lesson I learned during my undergraduate experience as a collegiate student athlete is balancing academics, athletics, and fun. If you engage in too many books or booze will not lead to a well-rounded learning experience.

ATHLETE 6

Name: Michael Stevenson

Sport(s) Played: Track and field

University Attended: Western Illinois University

Years Attended: 1983–1987

Undergraduate Degree: Bachelor of Science in Kinesiology

Highest Degree Obtained: Master of Science in Kinesiology

Parent(s) Occupation: Principal/teacher

Current Occupation: Head track and field coach

Ethnicity: White

Gender: Male

I chose my undergraduate institution for three main reasons: the cost of attendance, proximity to home, and the influence of Western Illinois University in the tri-state region of Illinois, Missouri, and Iowa. I was also familiar with Western Illinois' brand. I grew up knowing about this university. I began attending collegiate sporting events on campus as a middle school student, and learned to identify with this institution from an early age. Initially, I did not receive an athletic scholarship as a freshman. After my first year, I received a scholarship as a sophomore. I never considered transferring to another school for any reason.

The first semester was difficult for me. I struggled academically during that semester. I had one particularly difficult class that I was forced to drop because I was in over my head. In another class that I did poorly in primarily because it was boring class I had ever taken. I received my first poor grade in college. If you look at my college transcript, the first grade on my college transcript is a "D." The only one I ever received in my many years of schooling. I was embarrassed to say the least. This poor grade also provided me with a great deal of motivation to never let it happen again. I tried to use failures or setbacks as fuel to motivate me, and it seemed to work pretty well. During my first semester, I was pretty homesick and traveled home as often as I could. After my first semester, I made many new friends, and I began to feel more comfortable and began to enjoy my experience. It would have been great to step right into college and be confident, but it took about a semester to get fully adjusted. When I started college, I was unsure in my athletic endeavors as well. It was not until we began to have track meets and my performances were solid enough to earn some respect that I began to feel confident both athletically and academically a college level.

I was very fortunate to have a strong and support system at home. By earning a track and field scholarship after my first year, it helped relieve some of the financial burden. I had a good summer job earning about three times the minimum wage per hour and I worked about fifty hours a week. The combination of my scholarship and the money earned from my summer job took a load off of me financially. My parents assisted me with the small financial gap that was left. My parents gave me with a great deal of strength, so they had a big impact and influence on me. My coach also had a big impact on me.

Often, I was the only white athlete in races or the only white guy in my training group. I can only recall two incidents of racism during my undergrad experience. I do not think either experience had a dramatic effect on my experiences as an undergraduate experience. As far as institutional discrimination, I believe that many individuals, especially in the athletic arena, felt as though smaller schools are discriminated against. We would often note how our school was treated unfairly at certain events or contests due the fact because we were not at a school "Power 5" school.

It was so long ago that I went to school, I am not sure calendars were invented yet! I had to become more organized, so I relied heavily on a planner and calendar book that I purchased in the bookstore every fall. This was one of the strategies I used to successfully complete my undergraduate degree. I released that I studied better in the library because I removed myself from the social situations that were present in the residence hall or in my off-campus living. I think the biggest asset for student athletes is their ability to focus and have a better sense of time management than nonathletes regular people. Student athletes tend to be more disciplined in their approach to everything, partly because it is a requirement of sport. Another asset is the strong support system provided to student athletes. The advice is simple: be focused and determined in your approach to school work and athletic endeavors. Find a way to be passionate about what you are doing and appreciative of the opportunities you have.

I firmly believe that being a student athlete made me more grounded. I was more disciplined because of the sport. Practices or competitions used most of my "free time," so when I had time away from my sport I needed to use it wisely and spend it on my studies. While I still had a good social life, my sport kept me from potentially going down destructive paths due to the time commitment.

ATHLETE 7

Name: David McDaniel

Sport(s) Played: Football

University Attended: Western Illinois University

Years Attended: 2011–2015

Undergraduate Degree: Bachelor of Arts in Communication and a minor in Business

Highest Degree Obtained: Bachelor of Arts

Parent(s) Occupation: Liaison between Head Start Program and Southern Illinois University Edwardsville

Current Occupation: Part-time student worker for an athletic department

Ethnicity: Black

Gender: Male

I chose to attend Western Illinois University because it was far from enough away from home but just close enough to my surrounding family. It was because it would provide me with the potential to pursue a graduate degree in sports management after I completed my undergraduate studies. Western Illinois also competes in one of the best conference for Division 1A football conferences in the country; these were also major factors in choosing my undergraduate institution. Getting a scholarship offer also added motivation to come attend this university. Higher education is important to my family. My parents continuously expressed to the younger family members the importance of a college education. When we completed high school, it was an expectation for all of us to pursue a college education.

I became a key player in the football program by gaining the trust and confidence from my coordinator. After gaining his trust, I knew I could continue to be successful on the field. Our team lost a lot of games our team's sub-par seasons and as a result, I considered transferring. After thinking about it for a while, I determine that it was too big of a risk for me. There were several factors that helped me come to that conclusion. I considered the good support system that I had at the university from my defensive coordinator and peers. I realize that it was the best decision for me to remain and complete my athletic career and academic studies at this institution. I determined that be benefits outweighed the liabilities and getting my education paid for through my athletic scholarship was a better option than transferring to another school and starting over.

Transitioning to college was not as difficult as I imagined before I enrolled. My high school was one of the best in the state, so academics were not a problem for me. The hardest part of transitioning was trying to keep a healthy balance of social life, academics, and football all at the same time. Football always kept us on a pretty tight schedule with study tables and other tutorials. I believe that asking questions and asking for help from the support staff and my peers attributed to my success. A driven person knows that they cannot accomplish things alone. Successful people know how to ask for help.

It took some time to gain that confidence even though I always considered myself a confident person. When I came to Western Illinois University, I was not physically ready for Division 1 athletics. By the third game of my freshman season, I was eventually red-shirted. It was difficult to watch football for a whole year, not be part of the team but not compete. It was difficult to being red-shirted because it was difficult to practice every day and not play in a game. Being red-shirted did help me develop as a football player. The year after my red-shirt, I had a good game against the University of Missouri. This let me know that I could compete against the big school athletes.

The loans and scholarship were critical pieces that contributed to your success as an undergraduate student athlete. I am from a single parent household. My mom supported our family with a teacher's salary, so every dime from the school and government were important to being able to attend and complete college. Without the scholarship and loans there was not a chance I would have made it to college. My family and friends were the most important relationships as a student athlete. My mom and extended family were very supportive of my efforts. My family frequently called me to encourage me. They could not offer me money but their words of wisdom were better than anything that money could buy.

As an undergraduate athlete, I bonded with some of my professors. I also build a bond with some people on the staff at the university. I believe that we had mutual respect but never a deep connection. I met a lot of people who have helped me on my journey. From my coaches and coaches in other sports to the staff people in the athletic department; all of them have helped me in numerous ways that have gotten me to where I am now.

I have male privilege, so I do not believe that I was affected by gender discrimination. However, I did experience racial discrimination. I believe that I faced a lot of discrimination and outright racism from the institution as well as people, and police officers in the town where my institution is located. I believe that it is important for the local community that the college is to support their student athletes no matter their race, gender, or sexuality.

I approach college athletics like as a marathon and not as a sprint race. I have handled my disappointments like running in a marathon. I have looked at the long view. I also look at life just as a competing in football, you do not quit when you make a bad play because you still have to play. In my life, I have experienced many failures. Even with these failures, I believe I am extremely blessed. As an athlete, I could never just harp on my losses. I believe our losses also cannot go unnoticed, so all I could do as an athlete of student is strive to be better, and work harder. I used this as a lesson in life. My failures have taught what is important in life.

Through sports, I met people who genuinely cared about me. I met people who were on the same path of success just like me. College athletics opened my network tremendously. I have met people from all over the country and I am comfortable in all settings. College athletics kept me motivated and help my transition the lessons of determination, perseverance, and integrity learned on the field and in my daily life. Through college athletics, I have met some lifelong friends.

There is a great deal of knowledge that I have gained during my time as student athlete. I urge student athletes should take advantage of everything given to you. Student athletes should not leave any stone unturned. Not everyone gets a college education and the privilege of getting it paid for through a scholarship. Student athletes should use their time in college to experience so many things from collegiate sports, travel, diverse peers, and prevalent young minds everywhere, to help build your network and brand for the future.

Love, honesty, and integrity were big factors in getting through college athletics. I saw a lot of people dish out hate and do the wrong things. It appeared to me that it always came back around to them. As a student athlete, you will encounter all kinds of people. The worst thing a student athlete can do is make enemies and have low integrity because your peers and the community will notice.

ATHLETE 8

Name: Andrew

Sport(s) Played: Baseball

University Attended: Davidson College (Davidson, North Carolina)

Years Attended: 2007–2011

Undergraduate Degree: Bachelor of Science in Psychology with a minor in Philosophy

Highest Degree Obtained: Master of Science in Sport Psychology and Motor Behavior

Parent(s) Occupation: Father, dentist; mother, attorney

Current Occupation: Doctoral student at the University of Tennessee in Sport Psychology and Motor Behavior

Ethnicity: Caucasian

Gender: Male

I chose to attend Davidson College because it was an institution with a highly regarded academic reputation. It is an institution with a liberal arts reputation and a great academic pedigree. The decision really was a no brainer, it gave me the opportunity to play Division I baseball and obtain a degree at a great institution. I received athletic scholarship, but this was not a motivation for going to college. After I learned more about Davidson, my heart was set on this school. For me, the most difficult transition from high school to college was the adjustment to academic work. I attended a private college preparatory high school; I still found the strenuous academic rigor at Davidson a bit overwhelming. I am not sure that I could have been prepared for the balancing the high academic standards; especially with the amount of time occupied by baseball. I experienced initial athletic success. Even with this success, it took me some time to develop confidence in my skills as an academic.

I do not believe that I experience discrimination or racism at Davidson probably due to being a white male at a strong academic liberal arts school. Due to my parents' occupation, my financial circumstances were never an issue. There were many factors that contributed to my success. A change in position in baseball helped with my success and having a great support system made up of several people. Each of them helped me in different areas of my life. I was moved from a starting pitching to a closing pitcher, the one who comes in during the ninth inning, my junior year. It positively and directly affected my confidence in the classroom. In general, I have leaned on my family for support. When I had difficulty in the classroom, I leaned on the support staff and professors. When I had difficulty in the field, I leaned on my teammates and my pitching coach as a support system.

I used several strategies to complete my undergraduate degree. One of the most important strategies that I used was to study during the small breaks in my schedule during my day. I learned to use a spare ten or fifteen minutes during the day to stay connected to my studies. I realized that there were going to be very few times during the week when I would have hours to study. It is very important for student athletes to be efficient with their time. It is also important realized how to become efficient and take advantage of unaccounted time during the day.

I suggest that current or future student athletes to go to college for the right reasons. You should not go to school only for sports. I had the chance to play "pro" baseball in the minor league. No matter how good you are at a sport there will always be those much better than you. Go to a university that you connect with on levels beyond that of sport. Unless you have the athletic talent to be a blue-chip or five-star recruit playing basketball or football at a large FBS institution make sure you understand how collegiate athletics work. You will spend more time playing sports than studying and other commitments. I was a member of a fraternity as an undergraduate student. My fraternity's officers and members were lenient with me and other members who participated of college athletics. They allowed us to opt out of some fraternal duties. My fraternal obligations often conflicted with my athletic commitments.

Competing as a college athlete forced me to realize what is actually important. It made me manage my time and it gave me an appreciation for life outside of baseball. I believe it is essential that undergraduate student athletes understand that sport is important to a certain extent, but it is a far cry from being the most important. Sports at the end of the day are trivial. Sports are a zero-sum event. There is a winner and a loser and there is more to life than this. It is important to cherish the friends you make and the connections you cultivate. Getting good grades and having a good grade point average are what are important because they set open more doors of opportunities for you. As a college athlete, it is important to be the best that you can be and also learn the lessons sports so often teach us. Most important, take advantage of the time in college and build relationships with people in the general student population.

ATHLETE 9

Name: Ryan Demming

Sport(s) Played: Football

University Attended: Western Illinois University

Years Attended: 2009–2014

Undergraduate Degree: Law Enforcement and Justice Administration

Highest Degree Obtained: Master's Degree in Sports Management

Parent(s) Occupation: Retired military

Current Occupation: Graduate assistant

Ethnicity: Bahamian

Gender: Male

Coming out of high school, I was being recruited by several schools that were undergoing coaching changes. After all of the coaching changes at these schools and the end of the recruiting process, I had only one full scholarship offer. I accepted this offer because it would ease my financial burden of paying for college. If I had not received an athletic scholarship, I would have enrolled in the University of North Carolina Chapel Hill. My parents were not going to pay for college, so I was motivated to play sports to try to get a scholarship offer. I had the opportunity to transfer to another university, but I was very reluctant because I did not want to have to start over at another institution. I also did not want to have to figure out how a new school and athletic program operated.

I believe that my transition from high school to college was not very difficult for me because I am a military brat. I was accustomed to moving around or staying with other families for years at a time. I found having more freedom a little difficult. I had to learn how to use my time wisely. I was able to get a head start by going to football camp during the summer before all of the general student population came to campus. This helped me transition from high school to college easier than some other students. I was able to learn the campus buildings and how things worked without having the pressure of school assignments. I was able to get oriented to the campus about a month before school actually started. This familiarity made my transition easier.

I was red-shirted during my freshman year. Being red-shirted made me question my abilities; I wondered if my talent was up to par. I wondered if I had peaked as an athlete or if I would continue to develop as an athlete. I was fortunate that my coaches helped me with my confidence. They continued to encourage me and repeatedly told me that I would be a monster in this league. My coaches' words helped me believe I would dominate when I got the opportunity to compete in games. It was important for me to develop relationships with my teammates, classmates, and professors. I believe that it is all about who you know on campus to help you connect and accomplish whatever you want.

The issue of race is pervasive at a college. To me, the word "race" is funny word with a complex and varied meanings. Overcoming racial oppression is a day-to-day struggle. I have faced a two-edged sword of stereotyping. I believe some professors stereotype me and other blacks because of our race. I also believe I was stereotyped because I was a minority athlete. I have experienced dog whistle racism where on the surface it could not be seen or heard. Coaches and administrators made comments and sent racist subliminal messages. I feel sometimes those who hold power send messages of white supremacy. These messages came off as, "Never forget your position. Never forget we are not an equal. Never forget you need me to be successful. Never forget you are black and I am white."

I believe I have witnessed decisions being made because of race. During my undergraduate athletic career, I believe that some white athletes and coaches have been given opportunities that they did not earn. If people really do believe that people have opportunities that they do not deserve, I raise the following questions: "What percent of college coaches and professional coaches are minorities? What percentage of athletes are minorities?" You do not overcome a racist experience! I have become conscious of how much harder I and other black athletes have to work to become equal.

When it came to handling my school work, I found it difficult studying in the library or at a study table with other peers. I was easily distracted. I decided to lock myself in my room and work on projects and get them completed prior to their due dates. This worked for me. I wanted to stay on top of my work as much as possible. It was helpful to dedicate at least two hours every night to homework, but secluded in my own room.

I discovered that I needed to network with various people. Student athletes should network, but remain being their own person. Student athletes cannot rely on people handing them something because they may be a sports star. As a student athlete, you must work hard. You must actually give the effort to grasp the concepts and knowledge being taught in classes. By all means, do not just go through the motions in your classes. You must take advantage of learning. I also believe that participating in sports actually hurt my grade point average. Though it may have hurt my grade point average, college athletics opened doors for me that I would not have had as a general student in college.

ATHLETE 10

Name: Elizabeth Taylor

Sport(s) Played: Volleyball, track and field

University Attended: University of Wisconsin–Stevens Point

Years Attended: 2008–2011

Undergraduate Degree: Business Administration

Highest Degree Obtained: Master of Science in Kinesiology (Sport Psychology)

Parent(s) Occupation: Father, principal; mother, manager

Current Occupation: Doctoral student and instructor

Ethnicity: Caucasian

Gender: Female

I chose my undergraduate institution because I could become a multiple sport athlete in college. I wanted to play volleyball and run track. I did not receive an athletic scholarship, so the athletic program allowing me to compete in two sports was a big factor in deciding to attend University of Wisconsin at Stevens Point. I wanted to attend a smaller school with smaller classes and closer relationship with my professors. I also had an emotional connection to the school: my father was an alum of the school and it was close to my hometown, which allowed family and friends to come and see me compete. My family had financial resources to assist in paying for my undergraduate education, so this was not as stressful for me as some of my teammates.

Initially, I attended the University of Minnesota. At the University of Minnesota, I experienced extremely large classes and it appeared that my professors cared more about their research more than teaching students. Teaching assistants and graduate assistants taught most of the classes. I did like being taught by graduate students, so I decided to transfer to a smaller school (University of Wisconsin–Stevens Point) because it was a better fit for me.

To be a successful student athlete in the classroom, I took advantage of the resources that were provided by the athletic department. I attended study sessions and completing course readings prior to going to my classes. If I could not read it all, I was at least familiar with the main points of the readings. I completed a couple of internships and worked jobs on campus—all of these the elements contributed to my success as a student athlete. I also developed relationships with professors, and with coaches and administration in athletic department. My family, friends, and professors were all extremely important to me while completing my undergraduate education. Their influences were major contributors to my success as a student athlete.

I am a Type-A personality, I used a detailed daily planner to schedule all of my daily activities. I scheduled my study time. I scheduled my study table times, which was at least one night a week. I also organized group study meetings for exams and projects and found accountability partners to keep me accountable. One bit of advice I would offer student athletes: you should finish homework and class projects before you go out to socialize. It is important to remember to not procrastinate. Procrastination will negatively affect your academic success. If possible, I believe that student athletes should be involved in activities outside of sports. I was involved in extracurricular activities and organizations as a student athlete.

I was involved in a few organizations. I was a member of the Economics Club and the Human Resources Management Club. I was also a member of the Women in Business mentoring program, and the Student Athlete Advisory Committee. Being involved in extracurricular activities helped me be successful in my undergraduate studies. It helped me build relationships with like-minded students.

By competing in collegiate athletics, I built positive relationships. It also helped me learn to budget and prioritize my time. College athletics helped give me a purpose and an identity on campus. I think being a student athlete was one of the biggest reasons I was such a successful undergraduate student, and it definitely pushed me to attend graduate school. Athletics taught me so many life lessons: perseverance, focus, dedication, disappointment, and healthy relationships. I wish every student athlete could have as positive experience as I did as a Division III student athlete.

ATHLETE 11

Name: Kelsey Proctor

Sport(s) Played: Basketball

University Attended: Florida Atlantic University

Years Attended: 2011–2015

Undergraduate Degree: Bachelor of Science in Business Management with a minor in Marketing

Highest Degree Obtained: Bachelor of Science

Parent(s) Occupation: Mother, retired; father, sales person

Current Occupation: Graduate assistant

Ethnicity: Caucasian

Gender: Female

I first attended a junior college and then I transferred to a four-year institution. I decided to attend a junior college before going to a four-year school because I did not know what sport I wanted to continue. I could not decide if I wanted to continue playing basketball or volleyball. Going to a junior college gave me the opportunity to continue playing both sports for two more years.

After junior college, I chose Florida Atlantic University (FAU) based on multiple factors. One major factor was that I had a full ride scholarship offer to play basketball. I realize that I was very fortunate to get a scholarship. I understand these kinds of opportunities are not experienced by all student athletes. My scholarship paid for my tuition, books, room and board, meal plan, and all student fees. I am still extremely grateful for the scholarship. Another factor in my choosing FAU was their focus on academics. When I was on my recruiting trip, FAU coaches and advisors talked about the kind of education I would receive if I chose to attend the school. I felt very confident this school would give me the opportunity to get a degree from a good university. This university would also give me the tools to be a successful person. I also chose FAU because it would allow me to live in another state with a better climate. What Midwesterner would not want to attend to a university in Florida?

My parents think very highly of the educational process. If I would not have gotten a scholarship to play basketball, I believe they would have provided some type of support to help me pay for college. I believe my parents would have helped me secure a loan or pay back the loan after I graduated from college. Knowing that I would receive scholarship money allowed me to not worry about the cost of attending a college out of state.

For any incoming freshman student athlete, I believe that there is always a little doubt in the classroom and on the court. I know that I was extremely nervous because I was on my own for the first time. I had to take responsibility for my own actions. I had to do my assignments and turn them in by the deadlines. Having mandatory team study halls helped and removed any excuse not to finish assignments. My academic transition was not difficult. I felt as if my high school prepared me well for college. I did not struggle in my classes and my grades were good. My grades were so good that I became a member of the honor society Phi Theta Kappa.

I do not think that my racial identity affected my experience as an undergraduate student athlete. On my junior college team and at FAU, I was one of very few white girls on the team. At FAU the campus is very diverse. This diversity allowed me to grow and learn and experience other cultures. I do not think that my gender identity affected my experience either. I was a minority on campus and in my major but I did not experience any situations of discrimination. I had many important relationships as a student athlete. I depended on my family, best friend back home, and friends that I made outside of the basketball team. I also developed a friendship with my athletic advisor. I believe that it is important to develop relationships with people others people besides teammates. Even with the relationships and friendships I had developed, I still made numerous phone calls home to talk to my parents when I experienced adversity. When things were not going my way or I just felt defeated, my parents were always my first phone call for encouragement. My parents had a way of making me look for a silver lining and a brighter day. Usually, they simply reminded me how fortunate I was to receive a scholarship and compete on the Division I level. Even when school was tough, my parents guided me to see the positives. They urged me that I could not control everything and I could only worry about the things that I could not control.

I used several tools to keep organized with school and sports. I relied on my student planner. I made sure to look over all of the syllabi for my courses. I put everything in my student planner, so I knew what I had coming up and when I needed to be at certain places. I remained focused by scheduling a weekly meeting with my athletic-academic advisor because I participated in a high-risk sport. It was the university's policy that if student athletes competed in high-risk sports, it was mandatory to meet with her once a week. I also had to complete a certain amount of study hall hours per week. Having a tight schedule was very helpful because I had no excuse not to get my work done. When I first enrolled at FAU, I did not attend church very frequently. A few of my teammates attended church just about every Sunday, so I began going with them. It is easier to attend church during the off season, but once the season began it was more difficult because of our travel schedule. I would also attend the Fellowship of Christian Athletes when my class schedule allowed it. Student athlete should understand they are not invincible. The community, university, and others will hold you to a higher standard the general student population. Student athletes live in a fish bowl and if something happens with you, it may be blown out of proportion. Enjoy your time as a student athlete— it goes by really fast. I believe participating in collegiate athletics really helped prepare me for life after college. As a student athlete there are so many demands put on you. It is like having a full-time job and a part-time job at the same time.

Playing college basketball was one of the best experiences of my life. Sports, in particular basketball, taught me so many life lessons. I discovered that no one will make you show up or do your work for you. Collegiate sports taught me account-ability and not to let my teammates or myself down. I suggest student athletes use all of their resources. Study hall and study tables are not meant to be a punish-ment. Study hall and study tables are actually very helpful and they are there to help you succeed. Student athletes should meet with their athletic-academic advi-sor; they are there to help you to academically succeed. You should buy a planner and use it. Using a planner is not silly—it seems silly but it really helps you stay organized. I think many student athletes think that just because they are on schol-arship things will be handed to them. Many student athletes do not take advantage of the "mandatory seminars" that the athletic departments provide for them. Most student athletes do not realize they are being provided tools for their future, prob-ably more so than the average student gets. Future student athletes must take ad-vantage of all of the resources that are provided to them.

ATHLETE 12

Name: Anonymous

Sport(s) Played: Soccer (4 years) and softball (2 years)

University Attended: Pacific University

Years Attended: 2008–2012

Undergraduate Degree: Bachelor of Science in Exercise Science, minor in Psychology

Highest Degree Obtained: Master of Science in Exercise Science and Sport Studies

Parent(s) Occupation: Father, data processor; mother, U.S. Postal Service employee

Current Occupation: Doctoral student in Kinesiology, Recreation, and Sport Studies

Ethnicity: Japanese

Gender: Female

I chose to attend Pacific University because of its strong Exercise Science program. I also chose to attend Pacific University because the athletic department would allow me be a multiple sport athlete in soccer and softball. I did not receive an academic scholarship because Pacific is a Division III institution. These institutions do not give athletic scholarship money. My parents did a wonderful job of saving for my college education. They paid for my entire undergraduate degree and I did not have to work while I attended school. I did during the summers, and one spring.

I loved my experience at Pacific University. I liked the small class sizes and the ability to have relationships with my professors. I also really loved the location. The transition from high school to college was fairly smooth. Because I competed in a fall sport, we reported to school before the entire student body. I think this helped with my transition as I got to spend a lot of time with my teammates and get to know them before having to deal with attending classes. I also had a friend from my hometown who attended with me, and this definitely helped the transition process. Because many of my teammates and I had the same major, we were able to form study groups on road trips. We usually signed up for the same class schedules. My professors really knew me and helped me. This is a reason I loved going to a small school where I could build those relationships and feel comfortable with talking to my professors outside of the classroom setting.

Athletically, I knew I was in a place to be successful, especially after going through a few days of preseason. Academically, it definitely took some time to transition into good study habits and the rigor of the institution. My first two years of taking general education courses were challenging while I was playing two sports. We played almost all of our games on the weekend, so sometimes we would leave Friday morning and get back late Sunday night. I often felt that many of my big tests fell on the Monday after a long road trip, so it made preparing for those tests particularly difficult. As a college athlete, my schedule was regimented. It usually went like this; you wake up and you go to class. You study before practice if you have time, and then you go to practice. You eat and then you study.

After you complete everything on the schedule, you go to sleep. This was pretty much your schedule every day. This regimented schedule helped keep me on task and not be lazy. Playing two sports for two years was helpful. My last two years it was easy to find other things to do in my spare time. I primarily used a student planner.

I enrolled at Pacific University directly after high school. This was the first time in my 18 years where I did not necessarily feel like a racial minority. About one-third of the students who attend Pacific are from Hawaii and are therefore some form of Asian descent. It was a unique dynamic between those students from Hawaii and those from the "Mainland." I got the benefit of the doubt being both Asian, but also being from the Mainland, so I was accepted by both groups.

During my junior year as an undergraduate, Pacific University reinstituted the football program. It was not until this that I felt discriminated against as a female athlete. Football took precedence over every other sport and received benefits not afforded to other athletes. In addition, many students did not attend our games, and our final home game (Senior Day) was scheduled on a Friday at noon when many people are in class. The men's soccer team's (Senior Day) was on a Sunday like many of our other games throughout the season. Football's Senior Day would have never been scheduled on Friday or Sunday.

During my time as a student athlete, I was a part of the Student Athletic Advisory Committee for two consecutive years. I was president of this committee during my senior year. As committee president, I formed a relationship with Special Olympics Oregon and we raised $1,000 to fund two athletes for an entire year. Along with being president, I was on the College of Arts and Sciences Student Senate. I am not sure it helped me complete my undergraduate degree, but it helped me feel closer to the university and give back to the community.

Being a student athlete is hard, demanding, but it is so worth it. Rely on your family, friends, coaches, and professors to help support you when you need it. Take an interest in your academics, as they will often take you farther than your athletic career. Enjoy the moment—it goes by fast. I would advise student athletes to work hard and develop a strong work ethic. The tenacity, confidence, focus, support, drive that you learn by competing in sports is immeasurable. Collegiate athletics gave me structure and it enabled me to form many relationships. It gave me a family away from home. It gave me a sense of belonging. It also provided me with an opportunity to hone my knowledge, skills, and abilities taught me about communication, being a leader, and sport psychology.

ATHLETE 13

Name: Billy Wright

Sport(s) Played: Basketball

University Attended: Bradley University

Years Attended: 1992–1996

Highest Degree Obtained: Bachelor of Science

Current Occupation: Head basketball coach

Ethnicity: African American

Gender: Male

I chose my undergraduate institution, Bradley University, because it appeared to have everything that I wanted. It had a good academic reputation and they gave me an athletic scholarship with an opportunity to play my freshman year. Receiving a scholarship was also a major factor in me choosing Bradley. This scholarship also motivated me to stay in school; I am not sure that I would have been able to attend if I had not received a scholarship. I did not transfer to another school. From day one, I knew I had made the right decision because everything that I needed was at Bradley University.

I was confident when I began my college athletic career because I had had some success during my high school years. In high school, I had success both on the court and in the classroom. The most difficult transition for me was being away from the familiarity of home. I did find it difficult balancing the demands of college athletics and academics. The combination of receiving a scholarship and the structured environment that college athletics provided were very good for me. It helped me to develop self-discipline to complete my undergraduate studies. I believe that my most important relationships while as an undergraduate student were with my family and my teammates. I spent so much time with my teammates; I could not help but get close to them. I did not experience any racist incidents or any race-related problems at Bradley University. I truly enjoyed my time there.

I depended on my resilience to be successful as an athlete and a student. When I experienced any kind of disappointments or failures in the classroom or in competition, I gave myself positive affirmation through self-talk. I have always told myself to attempt to seek solutions and not seek excuses. During the tough times, I told myself I could become bitter or work harder and become better. I employed several strategies to stay organized and manage balancing work and athletics. I used an organizer and took advantage of study tables. I took my academics seriously. I made sure that I had an understanding of what readings and assignments required in all of my courses. I kept all of my exams because often professors would use some of the unit exam questions on final exams. This was very helpful because once you learned the information, you did not have to learn it twice.

I firmly believe that if you discipline yourself, you will not have to receive discipline from your coaches. Most of us know the difference between right and wrong. It is about making good choices, and you must make good choices. I also believe that student athlete should not allow hard work to discourage them from chasing their dreams. It may not happen according to your timetable. Patience is a good virtue. You may have to be patient before you accomplish your goals.

While an undergraduate student athlete, I met with a Fellowship Christian Association (FCA) representative. FCA employed representatives to minister not only to me but any athlete who was enrolled in athletics at Bradley University. I did not join a fraternity as an undergraduate. Athletics took up so much of my time that I could not have been a good member of an organization. Basketball was my organization; I was a member of Hooper Phi Hooper. I believe student athletes who want to be successful should be accountable and have discipline. Competing in basketball in college helped me to stay focused. As a scholarship student athlete, you have to maintain a certain grade point average, and matriculate toward graduation, and receive your degree.

ATHLETE 14

Name: Tori Niemann

Sport(s) Played: Basketball

University Attended: University of Missouri and Western Illinois University

Years Attended: Missouri University, 2010–2012; Western Illinois University, 2012–2015

Undergraduate Degree: Bachelor of Arts in Journalism

Highest Degree Obtained: Master of Science in Sport Management

Parent(s) Occupation: Construction company owner

Current Occupation: Athletic academic services

Ethnicity: White

Gender: Female

I chose the University of Missouri because I am from Missouri, so representing my home state was a big draw. I immediately connected with the basketball team and its family atmosphere. Later, I transferred from the University of Missouri to Western Illinois University. There were several factors that went into my decision to transfer. I did not believe that I could be successful at Missouri and I wanted to be a part of a different athletic program with an opportunity to win and be successful. I transferred to Western Illinois University because I had a prior relationship with the coaching staff and I knew they would believe in me. At WIU, they were rebuilding the program, and I believed that I had a chance to make an impact.

I was on scholarship at both universities I attended. I knew that I would attend college regardless of playing a sport and receiving an athletic scholarship. At first, the transition was difficult in trying to find a balance between freedom and the Division I athletic demands. I attended summer session before my first college fall semester, so that made the transition much easier with only two classes and a much smaller student population.

College athletics gave me a great opportunity. I received so much support from athletic personnel. I had a full-ride scholarship. I had tutors, trainers, and mentors to help me to succeed as an athlete and student. I also had a lot of support from family. The support of my family was the most important to me. I also include my teammates as a part of my family. Your teammates are the ones you experience every emotion and almost every moment of your day with. In most cases, they can relate to your struggles and provide support that no one else can.

As a student athlete, I never experienced any incidents of racism or discrimination. If anything, I felt that I was judged as a student athlete. Many people make inaccurate assumptions about student athletes. Because I was a student athlete, some people assumed I had it easier than other students or I was not as intelligent as others. Some people even assumed that I was a lesbian because I was a college athlete.

I handled my disappointments or failures in the classroom and on the field of competition by using them as an opportunity to learn. Like most good athletes, I made adjustments and worked harder to get better. I made sure I did not make the same mistake twice. I made adjustments by taking a different approach to note taking and shooting 200 extra free-throws each week. I used a planner for each day, including classes, practices, study times, and even when to eat. Being organized each day helped me get everything done in an efficient manner.

I think it is important for student athletes to develop strong relationships with their teammates, coaches, athletic staff, and community members. They should remember there are very few people who have the opportunity to be a Division I student athlete, so be grateful and work hard. I think it is also important student athlete get involved in activities outside of athletics. I got involved of some activities outside of athletics. I was a member of the Student Athlete Advisory Committee, but no other organizations. I believe this group helped me find a voice and have a say about the use of student athletes' time. I also attended church throughout my college career. I attended church more frequently during my last year. I attended Fellowship of Christian Athletes at Western Illinois University, and our team organized Bible study at the University of Missouri.

It is important for student athletes to develop strong relationships. I developed strong relationships with many people that I may not have encountered as just a student. It is important to utilize the resources, such as extra academic support and the relationships with coaches and trainers. Student athletes have many people in their corner helping them along their college careers in terms of school, sport, career, and personal life.

ATHLETE 15

Name: Matt

Sport(s) Played: Baseball

University Attended: Western Illinois University

Years Attended: 2011–2013

Undergraduate Degree: Bachelor of Arts in History

Highest Degree Obtained: Master of Science in Sport Management

Parent(s) Occupation: Father, logistics manager; mother, recreation employee

Current Occupation: Assistant baseball coach

Ethnicity: Caucasian

Gender: Male

I chose Western Illinois University because I wanted to continue to play baseball at the highest level, after I completed my associate's degree in junior college. I transferred from Heartland Community College. I knew I wanted to continue to play baseball at the highest level. Western Illinois University seemed to be the right fit for me financially and athletically. Receiving a scholarship offer also factored in my college choice.

My first semester was difficult academically. I was fine being away from home because I was surrounded by classmates who were in the same situation. We were getting the opportunity to do what we loved to do in playing baseball. Academically, I was not acclimated to the style of teaching in a few of my courses. I believe this contributed to my academic difficulty. I was barely eligible for my first spring season. This was an eye-opening experience for me. During the spring semester, I developed a time management system on my own and used some of the resources at the institution, which helped me grow up and use the little time I had being a student athlete more efficiently. Athletically, I succeeded in the fall and spring. I devoted more time than ever before at playing baseball and I learned more about the game in that first year than I did in all of my previous years of playing baseball.

I received a full tuition scholarship both at Heartland Community College and at Western Illinois University. I managed my money pretty well. I had summer jobs and I was conservative in my spending, so I never felt like I was destitute. I believe finding a balance between being a student and athlete was a key to my success. I cherish the experience that I had with my teammates. I have great memories both on and off of the field.

I never ran into any problems with racism. Most of the guys I played with were Caucasian, but we had a few Hispanics, Asians, and African Americans. We always viewed ourselves as teammates and would do anything for one another. Race did not matter to us. I handled my classroom and athletic failures as a learning experience to become a better person. I knew that the four years in college were going to shape me into who I would become. Baseball is a unique game because you fail more than you succeed and it can still be considered a great success. I developed as a person greatly from learning how to handle failure and using it as a positive experience. Student athletes should not be too proud to ask for assistance. There is a big reason universities offer so many resources for student athletes, so take advantage of them.

I recommend student athletes approach their teammates and stay in constant contact with their coaches if they feel they are not up to speed in any area of their life; this includes social aspects, academics, or athletics. All student athletes must understand that it is a privilege to be a college athlete. There are millions of students who would do anything to be in a student athlete's position, but were not fortunate enough to make it to the collegiate level. That is why it's good to take advantage of the opportunity. It is important to stay in the present moment. This helps you to focus in on one task at a time. Far too many student athletes are worried about the future and if they will go pro. Being able to stay present and taking it day by day will help them stay focused on tasks and enjoy the experience.

It was important to me to do well in all my classes. It was the driving force for me doing well academically. Athletics and academics go hand and hand. It contributed to my overall contentment. I noticed when I did well in the classroom; I also played well on the field. Since I became a college baseball coach, it seems to be normal that my most successful players have also been our most academically successful students. Student athletes use their time to not only to develop into a better athlete, but also to develop a skillset that will help them stand out from others. Student athletes should learn from their mistakes and use their experiences to become a successful person.

ATHLETE 16

Name: Allison

Sport(s) Played: Softball

University Attended: Manhattan College and Wingate University

Years Attended: 2010–2014

Undergraduate Degree: Bachelor of Arts in Communications

Highest Degree Obtained: Master of Arts in Sport Administration

Parent(s) Occupation: Father, electrical crew manager; mother, IT specialist

Current Occupation: Doctoral graduate assistant

Ethnicity: Caucasian

Gender: Female

Coming out of high school, I went to Manhattan College. I transferred to Wingate because it gave me a better opportunity to play softball in college on scholarship. Out of high school, I was already motivated to go to college, but getting a scholarship allowed me to go to a private college.

My transition from high school to college may have been a little unique. I chose a university in New York City and nine hours from my hometown. Adjusting to life in New York City was an enormous adjustment for a girl from a small rural town. Academically, I was prepared and I did well at both Manhattan College and Wingate University. Athletically, it was a huge adjustment to have so many competing demands on my life for practice, training, and balancing academic and athletic demands. I struggled my freshman year at Manhattan and actually went through a period where I thought about quitting. I decided that I would transfer rather than quit. Once I transferred to Wingate, I believed that I was in a better environment that was a better fit for me. Initially, I was not sure how my family would feel about me transferring. My family was very supportive when I transferred schools and this was very important to me.

I think my relationship with my advisor and department chair was very valuable in my growth as a student. He became a valuable mentor and he still is my mentor. I regularly seek him out for advice while pursuing my doctoral studies. His advice has been invaluable in helping me navigate through my graduate courses and dissertation. Sometimes advisors try to push athletes into majors that may not be as challenging. It is our choice to choose the major that is best for us. I did not get pigeonholed into picking a major I did not want to do.

I did not personally face any racial or gender discrimination but I do think my university showed favoritism to some of the male sports programs. Each year our team requested funding for new lights for our field. The university's athletic program denied our team's requests; however, the football team received lights and a new field house. I handled disappointments by analyzing my mistakes and determining what went wrong and then allowing it to motivate me to improve next time. My failures have always been a way to push me throughout my life. I used an agenda and lists to keep up with my work and assignments. I also used a calendar to schedule study time every day after practice to keep myself on tasks.

As an athlete, you should enjoy the entire experience. Enjoy your teammates, the wins and the losses, because it will be over before you know it. Do not slack off—this could be costly. Give everything you have to your sport, i.e., effort, time, nutrition, and practice. Give everything in pursuing your degree also. Find a way to stay focused and keep yourself on task. Make time management a priority. It goes a long way in balancing all things that student athletes have to do. I did not attend religious services while in college and I was not in a sorority. My extracurricular activities consisted of being a writer and editor of the student paper. I held memberships in the Student Athlete Club, the Bulldog Club, and the communications organization. These organizations helped me network and find leads with job opportunities. I think college athletics kept me focused and disciplined. I never missed class. I kept up and on top of my assignments and classes.

ATHLETE 17

Name: Terri Anderson

Sport(s) Played: Track and field

University Attended: Purdue University

Years Attended: 2007–2012

Undergraduate Degree: Bachelor of Arts in Law and Society

Highest Degree Obtained: Master of Science in Sports Management

Parent(s) Occupation: Father, unemployed; mother, retired physical education teacher and an emergency medical technician

Current Occupation: Graduate assistant track and field coach

Ethnicity: Caucasian

Gender: Female

When I chose where I would go to college, I decided I would base my decision on good coaching. Finding a good coach was a major part of my decision where I would attend college. I was looking for a coach that would make me throw far and improve my technique. I knew it would take a little time to get adjusted to a new coach, new routine, and new training routine. I knew I would succeed because I was confident in my skills. I also knew it would take time to reach my maximum abilities as a Division I athlete.

When I enrolled in college, I had no clue what I wanted to study as my major or minor. I had set goals throughout high school. My top goal was to earn a full-ride scholarship for track and field. My parents were not able to pay for under-graduate education, so I knew I had to get a full scholarship offer in order to go to college. I had multiple scholarship offers from multiple athletic programs. Purdue University offered me a scholarship.

Academically, the transition was not too difficult. I did have a few difficult classes. I was naturally talented in academics in high school and I did not have to study much. As a result I had poor study habits when I arrived in college. I treated the collegiate academics like high school. I sat in most of my classes to listen to the professors and took notes. I do not recommend this as a method, but it worked for me. In some classes I did not even crack a book. I returned many books to the bookstore. The books were still in the protective plastic they came in.

During my freshman year, we were required to do eight hours a week of study hall. This requirement was helpful because it provided a place for me to get work done. My grades were never as good as they could have been. As a result, I was required to attend study hall and subject to grade checks. I did the bare minimum to get by and be eligible to compete in track and field. I had a very low standard in the classroom. Thus, I was rarely disappointed with my mediocre performance in the classroom. There are two classes that I found very difficult. I had trouble in an anthropology class. I believe that it was the hardest class I ever took. Another class that was difficult for me was a religion course. This course was not difficult on the surface. I struggled with the concept of religion and how it is used in America. As I look back at my time as a student athlete, I realize that if I had applied even one-fourth of the effort into academics as I did to athletics, I would have had much more success academically. I stayed motivated because if I had lost my scholarship, I would not have been able to continue my college education. If I did not stay eligible in school there would be not be any track and field.

Athletically, I was a little arrogant when I went to college. I thought I was hot stuff. I thought I was the best, and I was the best no matter who I competed against. I received a rude awakening! I was naturally talented athletically. I did not have to work hard athletically in high school. I found college athletics much more difficult. One of the biggest differences was the higher level of competition. I went from competing mostly in local and state with a few nationwide track and field competitions to all nationwide competitions. In college, I began to compete against other athletes who were just as talented as me or more talented than me. I went from a big fish in a little pond to a little fish in a big pond. The workouts were totally different. There were more hours devoted to practice. It was very difficult to figure out how to balance practice and academics. I struggled trying to give 100 percent to classes, homework, study tables, and domestic chores. Then on top of this, I tried to have some semblance of a social life. I found it all kind of difficult.

Having a good support system was extremely important me. I had a good support system as an undergraduate student athlete. It consisted of friends, family, advisers, and professors. My best friend was a major support person in my life. She was also involved in sports as a track and field athlete also. She attended a junior college in my hometown and competed in the pole vault. She quit because lost the love of the sport. My mom was also a big supporter and another link in my support system. I knew she was proud of me. She bragged about my athletic feats all the time. She traveled to damn near all of my track meets while I was in college. Once when I made it to nationals, my mom drove overnight to watch me compete, and the car did not have cruise control. I did not have a very good competition, but I was appreciative that she came to see me compete.

One of the most important links in my support system was my academic-athletic advisor, Tanya Foster. I might not be here today if it was not for her. She was so patient with me. There were so many times that I sat in her office and just cried. To this day, she is one of the most influential people in my life. She saw qualities in me that nobody else identified in me. I call her my life advisor. When I have a problem or issue, she is still one of the first people I call. Even her daughters and I have become close friends.

Another person in my support system as a student athlete was one of my professors, Patrick Jones. Pat is retired military as well as a decorated forensic scientist, analyst, and investigator. He was a huge influence on me. During my senior year, I was featured in an article in the student newspaper. Pat cut out the article and asked me to sign it, and then he laminated it and hung it in his office. This meant the world to me and motivated me to strive for higher heights.

I do not know if I experienced racial discrimination but some of my African American teammates would tease me about being "ghetto." I am a fairly large woman, so I had to make adjustments with my university-issued athletic wear. This sometimes caused me to be the butt of jokes. I wore sweats and shorts most of the time and because my legs are so long, I would sag my sweats so that my pants would not be above my ankles. One of my teammates told me that "I was the most ghetto white girl they ever met." The comments did not offend me, but it did make me think a few things.

In regards to gender discrimination, some of the males on the track team made sexist comments such as, "That's woman's work" or make references about "A man's work." I believe some of the most egregious discrimination and just sheer ignorance came from a coach. There was also a theory that females compete better when menstruating because of the surge of hormones. I had one coach who would make us track our periods and report to him. If we had any changes without birth control we were supposed to report this as well. He also wanted all athletes to report sexual activity. He believed there were certain time frames that sex affected our performance.

I also remember an incident where I felt disrespected because I am a woman. One of the male athletes on the track team was a member of a fraternity. He invited me and a couple of other female athletes to a fraternity party. At this party, I felt like a piece of meat. I certainly learned a lesson about the ills of fraternity culture on that night.

The only true advice I can give to future student athletes is to be true to yourself. There will be people who try to make you into someone that you are not. Do not allow people to influence you to become someone you are not proud of being. You must be able to look yourself in the mirror and feel good about who you see and the things you have done. I was viewed as an outcast by my teammates because I refused to degrade others and I did not have a negative attitude. I chose to be the best human being I could be. This was the best decision I made during my collegiate career.

Being a student athlete is an amazing experience. It is a once-in-a-lifetime opportunity. The four or five years are such a small amount of time in the overall length of your lifetime. There is more to life than just athletics. I think student athletes need to be driven, and determined, hardworking, strong willed, coachable, personable, and passionate. Notice none of these are actual athletic skills. Being a successful student athlete is so much more than the competition and athletic achievements. I owe much of my success to being a college student athlete but I am working on developing my personal identity outside of sports.

Index

About the Authors

Algerian Hart is an associate professor and graduate coordinator in the Kinesiology Department at Western Illinois University. He is the author of numerous articles and is the author of *Neglected Voices: Division I Student-Athletes' Perceptions of the NCAA Rules and Regulations* (Western Society for Kinesiology and Wellness: Monograph Series, 2008). He has extensive experience as an athlete and coach at the collegiate level.

F. Erik Brooks is a professor and chair of the Department of African American Studies at Western Illinois University. He holds a doctorate in public policy and administration from the L. Douglas Wilder School of Government and Public Affairs at Virginia Commonwealth University.